ACE Certified Personal Trainer Exam Prep

A concise study guide that highlights the key concepts required to pass the American Council on Exercise CPT Exam to become a certified personal trainer.

➤ Includes *"Key Concepts"* with the required information needed for the exam.

➤ Includes quick reference pages for helpful resources, formulas, conversions, and acronyms.

➤ Includes 50 practice questions to further enhance knowledge and to have an idea of what the actual exam will look like.

➤ Includes detailed practice question answers with explanations on how the answers were obtained.

➤ Includes detailed descriptions of assessments, the heart, muscles, nutrition, term definitions, training modalities, and more.

Study while on the go with ACE Audio Prep! It's a great supplement to this study guide that goes chapter-by-chapter pointing out all of the key information. Available on Amazon, Audible, and iTunes. Scan the QR code below with a smartphone camera to begin listening ↓

Follow us @CPTPrep
Contact info@cptprep.com

Access additional tips and resources at www.cptprep.com

Table of Contents

Table of Contents

Table of Contents

Table of Contents

Table of Contents

Table of Contents

Our Story...

My name is Daniel Hile and I'm the founder of CPT Prep. CPT Prep is a test preparation company that was created to help aspiring trainers become certified fitness professionals. The idea for CPT Prep started with a simple question that I asked myself after taking my first personal trainer exam...

What would have been helpful for me while I was preparing?

After preparing for the exam for a few months, reading the textbook, and taking notes. I scheduled and took the exam. I passed, but the test was tougher than I expected. I looked back at the pass rates for the exam, and at the time it was only 55%. I started to think about the other 45% of people who paid for the exam and study materials but didn't pass. The personal trainer textbooks can be overwhelming, and it's often unclear what to focus on while studying. That one question sent me down a path of compiling my notes, researching, and attempting to distill down the key information required to become a certified personal trainer. Every product that we have made including our *Study Guides, Audio Prep,* and each *Blog* that I have written has that same original goal in mind. It's a retrospective question *"What would have been helpful for me while I was preparing?"*

Our *ACE Certified Personal Trainer Audio Prep* is a great supplement to this study guide. It goes chapter-by-chapter pointing out all of the key information from *The Exercise Professional's Guide to Personal Training.* It's available on *Amazon, Audible, and iTunes.* The majority of the exam tests you on your practical / applied knowledge rather than specific memory recall. Combining the learning styles of *Audio, Visual, and Kinesthetic* will help you fully absorb the information so it can be applied during the exam and into your career as a fitness professional.

A lot of the information in the text is better understood when combined with a visual explanation or element *(especially with the anatomy of the body and assessments)*. We reference external resources that we have found helpful including *blogs, videos, pictures, apps, and fitness accounts*. There is a blog on our website titled *"Personal Trainer Resources"* that has every reference mentioned → **www.cptprep.com/single-post/resources**

We appreciate you checking us out and hope you find these tools helpful along your journey to becoming a certified fitness professional! We value your time and will help you make the most of it while preparing. If you have any questions or would like a topic covered in more detail please send us an e-mail at **info@cptprep.com**

~ CPT Exam Prep Team

ACE Certified Personal Trainer Performance Domains

Domains are listed below with the percentage of questions out of the 150 multiple-choice questions on the test. You are scored on 125 out of the 150 questions on the test. Out of the 125 graded questions, you must correctly answer approximately 90 questions for a passing score of 500 or better out of a possible 800 points.

Domain I*: Interviews and Assessments – 23% (29+/- Questions)*

Domain II*: Program Design and Implementation – 31% (39+/- Questions)*

Domain III*: Program Modification and Progression – 26% (32+/- Questions)*

Domain IV*: Professional Conduct, Safety, and Risk Management – 20% (25+/- Questions)*

ACE Certified Personal Trainer Test Statistics

2019: 20,069 candidates took the test with a pass rate of 71%
(14,249 passed / 5,820 failed)

2018: 22,923 candidates took the test with a pass rate of 70%
(16,046 passed / 6,877 failed)

2017: 20,129 candidates took the test with a pass rate of 65%
(13,084 passed / 7,045 failed)

This study guide was written to help enhance the knowledge required to become an ACE Certified Personal Trainer (CPT) and to give you the confidence that you are prepared come test day. Once you become certified this guide can be used to reference important information as you begin your career as a personal trainer.

Domain Breakdown by Chapters in The Exercise Professional's Guide

Domain I - Interviews and Assessments

Information for this Domain is found in Chapters 3, 4, 5, 7, 8, and 10.

This domain is dedicated to everything you would do with a client prior to beginning a program. This domain is all about gathering information to develop a program that best serves the *goals, needs, and abilities* of the individual client.

Domain II - Program Design and Implementation

Information for this Domain is found in Chapters 2, 6, 8, 9, and 11.

Domain II interprets the information that has been collected in Domain I, and uses it to make the MOST appropriate program for the individual client. This is where a key understanding of the 3 Phases of the *ACE Integrated Fitness Training (IFT) Model* comes into play. *Chapter 11 Integrated Exercise Programming: From Evidence to Practice* is a GREAT review of these chapters because it takes theoretical case studies and walks you through their program from beginning to end.

Domain III - Program Modification and Progression

Information for this Domain is found in Chapters 12, 13, 14, and 15.

Domain III takes everything you've learned up to this point where you're training an apparently healthy client, and then incorporates the important information on obesity, chronic diseases, exercise considerations across the lifespan, and considerations for clients with musculoskeletal issues.

Domain IV - Professional Conduct, Safety, and Risk Management

Information for this Domain is found in Chapters 1 and 16.

This domain is dedicated to being aware of what is within your scope of practice, knowing what your responsibilities are as a personal trainer *(professional and legal),* and the proper course of action to take when something goes wrong *(risk-management).*

Domain I: Interviews and Assessments

Develop rapport with clients to obtain relevant health and lifestyle information necessary for successful program design and outcomes.

Client Consultation Forms

➢ **Informed consent** *(assumption of risk)*

➢ **Liability waiver**

➢ **Physical activity readiness questionnaire (PAR-Q)**

➢ **Health-history questionnaire** *(Medical history, medications, supplements, exercise history, illnesses or injuries, lifestyle information such as nutrition, stress, work, sleep)*

➢ **Exercise history and attitude questionnaire** *(important for developing goals and designing programs)*

➢ **Medical release** *(if necessary once risk stratification has been completed)*

➢ **Testing forms** *(used to record testing and measurement data during the fitness assessment)*

➢ **Client-Personal trainer agreement** *(Agreement to participate)*

Preparticipation Physical Activity Screening Guidelines

➢ Identify those with medical *contraindications (exclusion criteria)* for performing physical activity.

➢ Identify those who should receive a medical/physical evaluation/exam and clearance prior to performing a physical activity program.

➢ Identify those who should participate in a medically supervised physical activity program.

➢ Identify those with other health / medical concerns.

Self-Guided Screening: An individual who is looking to become more physically active fills out a *Physical Activity Readiness Questionnaire (PAR-Q)* without direct input from a fitness professional.

ePARmed-X+Physician Clearance Follow-Up Questionnaire: A tool that a physician can use to refer individuals to a professionally supervised physical activity program and make recommendations for that program.

Professionally Supervised Screening: Involves an individual seeking guidance from a fitness professional to determine their physical readiness for exercise. This may involve collecting a *Health-History Questionnaire (HHQ)* along with a medical examination and clearance *(if warranted)*.

Preparticipation Physical Activity Screening is based on the following (3) factors:

1. The individual's current level of physical activity.
2. Presence of signs, symptoms, and/or known cardiovascular, metabolic, or renal disease.
3. Desired exercise intensity.

Cardiovascular, Metabolic, and/or Renal disease (CMR)

- Heart attack
- Heart surgery, cardiac catheterization, or coronary angioplasty
- Pacemaker/implantable cardiac defibrillator/rhythm disturbance
- Heart valve disease
- Heart failure
- Heart transplantation
- Congenital heart disease *(congenital refers to birth)*
- Diabetes, Type 1 and 2
- Renal disease such as renal *(kidney)* failure

Major Signs and Symptoms Suggestive of (CMR)

- Pain or discomfort in the chest, neck, jaw, arms, or other areas that may result from ischemia or lack of oxygenated blood flow to the tissue, such as the heart.
- Shortness of breath *(Dyspnea)* at rest or with mild exertion.
- Syncope *(loss of consciousness)*, fainting, and dizziness during exercise may indicate poor blood flow to the brain due to inadequate cardiac output from a number of cardiac disorders.
- Orthopnea refers to trouble breathing while lying down. Paroxysmal nocturnal dyspnea refers to difficulty breathing while asleep. Both are indicative of poor left ventricular function.
- Ankle edema *(swollen ankles)* that is not due to injury is suggestive of heart failure, a blood clot, insufficiency of the veins, or a lymph system blockage.
- Palpitations or tachycardia *(unpleasant awareness of the forceful or rapid beating of the heart)* may be induced by various disorders of cardiac rhythm.
- Intermittent claudication refers to severe calf pain when walking. This pain indicates a lack of oxygenated blood flow to the working muscles similar in origin to chest pain.
- Heart murmurs *(unusual sounds caused by blood flowing through the heart)* may indicate valvular or other cardiovascular diseases.
- Unusual fatigue or shortness of breath that occurs during light exertion or normal activity and not during strenuous activity. These may be benign or could indicate the onset of or change in the status of cardiovascular and/or metabolic disease.

If an individual has any signs or symptoms suggestive of CMR they should obtain medical clearance before beginning an exercise program regardless of their current exercise status.

The first step is to determine if the individual ***participates in regular exercise***. Defined as ***30 minutes of moderate-intensity activity at least 3 days per week for at least 3 months.*** Depending on the answer ***"Yes"*** or ***"No"*** the client is then put into that category and screened according to the recommendations below.

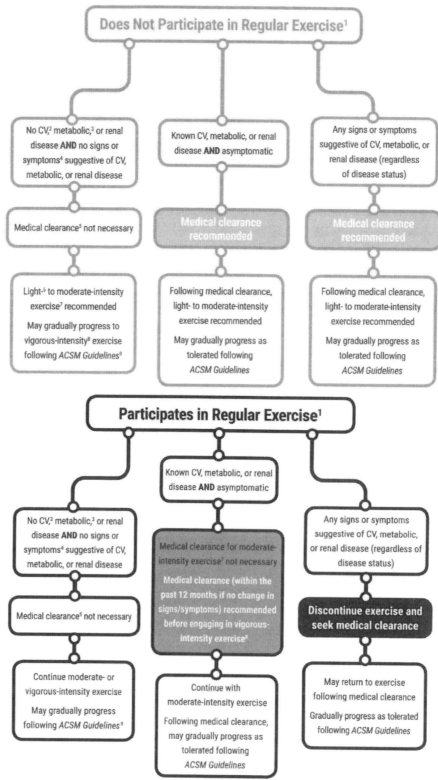

Risk Factors

Age: Men ≥45 years old, women ≥55 years old

Family History: Myocardial infarction *(heart attack)*, coronary revascularization *(bypass surgery or angioplasty)*, or sudden cardiac death before 55 years old in father or other male first-degree relative or before 65 years old in mother or other female first-degree relatives.

Cigarette Smoking: Current cigarette smoker or those who quit within the previous 6 months or exposure to secondhand tobacco smoke.

Sedentary Lifestyle: Not participating in at least 30 minutes of moderate-intensity physical activity *(40% to <60% VO$_2$R)* on at least 3 days of the week for at least 3 months.

Obesity: BMI *(Body Mass Index)* ≥30 or waist girth >102cm *(40 inches)* for men and >88 cm *(35 inches)* for women

Hypertension: Systolic blood pressure ≥140 mm Hg and/or diastolic ≥90 mm Hg, confirmed by measurements on at least two separate occasions, or on antihypertensive medication.

Dyslipidemia: Low-density lipoprotein cholesterol ≥130 mg or high-density lipoprotein cholesterol <40 mg or on lipid-lowering medication. If total serum cholesterol is all that is available, use ≥200 mg.

Prediabetes: Impaired fasting glucose = fasting plasma glucose ≥100 mg and ≤125 mg or impaired glucose tolerance = 2 h values in oral glucose test ≥140mg and ≤199 mg confirmed by measurements on at least two separate occasions.

Negative Risk Factor: High-density lipoprotein (HDL) cholesterol ≥60 mg
If any other risk factors are present this nullifies or takes one away.

\> Greater than
≥ Greater than or equal to
< Less than
≤ Less than or equal to

Having one or none of these Risk Factors indicates a low risk of future cardiovascular disease, whereas two or more risk factors indicate an increased risk for disease.

Absolute Contraindications

The risks of exercise testing outweigh the potential benefit. The client should not participate in exercise testing until conditions are stabilized or treated.

- Significant change in resting ECG.
- Unstable angina *(chest pain)*
- Uncontrolled cardiac dysrhythmias
- Severe symptomatic aortic stenosis
- Uncontrolled symptomatic heart failure
- Acute pulmonary embolus or pulmonary infarction
- Acute myocarditis or pericarditis
- Suspected or known dissecting aneurysm
- Acute systemic infection, accompanied by fever, body aches, or swollen lymph glands

Relative Contraindications

The benefits of exercise outweigh the risk. Exercise testing can be done only after careful evaluation of the risk/benefit ratio.

- Left main coronary stenosis
- Moderate stenotic valvular heart disease
- Electrolyte abnormalities
- Severe arterial hypertension
- Tachydysrhythmia or bradyarrhythmia *(fast or slow heart rate)*
- Hypertrophic cardiomyopathy and other forms of outflow tract obstruction
- Neuromuscular, musculoskeletal or rheumatoid disorders that are exacerbated by exercise
- High-degree atrioventricular block
- Ventricular aneurysm
- Uncontrolled metabolic disease
- Chronic infectious disease
- Mental or Physical impairment leading to inability to exercise adequately.

Certain medications or drugs may affect a client's ability to perform or respond to exercise. *Table 5-1 on page 151 of the Exercise Professional's Guide to Personal Training* describes the effects medications have on the heart-rate response. Any client taking medication that could potentially have an effect on exercise should have a physician's clearance for physical activity.

Although regular physical activity increases the risk of musculoskeletal injury and cardiovascular problems the overall physical activity risk in the general population is low, especially compared to the health benefits of regular exercise.

Physiological Benefits of Regular Exercise

- ➤ Improvement in cardio and respiratory function
- ➤ Reduction in coronary artery disease risk factors
- ➤ Decreased morbidity and mortality
- ➤ Decreased risk of falls
- ➤ Increased metabolic rate
- ➤ Improvement in bone health
- ➤ Weight loss and reduced obesity

Psychological Benefits of Regular Exercise

- ➤ Decreased anxiety and depression
- ➤ Enhanced feelings of well being
- ➤ Positive effect on stress
- ➤ Better cognitive function

Regular exercise is a key component of long-term weight management. The following is a list of benefits that exercise has in effective weight loss, and maintaining a healthy weight:

1) Exercise enhances daily caloric expenditure
2) Exercise, especially strength training, can minimize the loss of lean body mass.
3) Exercise may suppress appetite and counteract the impact that diet may have on resting metabolic rate (RMR).
4) Exercise makes the body more efficient at burning fat.

Adults should engage in at least ***150 minutes of moderate-intensity or 75 minutes of vigorous-intensity aerobic physical activity or a combination of both each week*** to improve overall health and fitness. Additional health benefits are obtained by performing more than 150 minutes of activity each week which also helps to further assist and maintain weight loss.

Overweight and obese individuals seeking to manage their weight should perform at least ***300 minutes of moderate-intensity or 150 minutes of vigorous-intensity exercise or activity or a combination of both each week.***

The daily amount of exercise can be performed in one continuous bout or broken up into smaller sessions of at least 10 minutes or more throughout the day.

Trainers should place the needs and abilities of their clients first and progress to the recommended weekly training durations only when suitable for the client, based on their conditioning level, tolerance, and availability.

Creating Personalized Training Programs

Your ***primary responsibility as a personal trainer*** is to design a training program that meets your client's ***Goals, Needs, and Abilities.*** This is accomplished through gathering and understanding the following three pillars of information:

1. **Assessments**

   ➤ **Subjective** assessments are used to obtain information about a client's personal history, as well as their occupation, lifestyle, and medical background. This includes gathering some initial client consultation forms such as *Health History Questionnaire, PAR-Q, and risk factors.*

   ➤ **Objective** assessments are **observations** that can be directly measured and quantified by the fitness professional. This includes *resting heart rate, blood pressure, posture, and movement assessments.* ****Think observable and measurable.***

2. **Human Movement Science** including *(anatomy, biomechanics, and motor behavior)*

3. **Training Principles** involve applying the *acute variables such as sets, reps, resistance, intensity, and rest periods along with the Principle of specificity and overload principle.*

The first step is to gather ***subjective assessment*** information during the initial client consultation. The next step is to determine the client's current ***postural stability, joint mobility, functional movement capacity, balance, cardiorespiratory fitness level, and muscular fitness.*** These are the ***objective assessments*** that can be ***observed.*** The ACE IFT model allows the option to either conduct evidence-based fitness assessments or lead clients through early training sessions that incorporate exercises and movements that provide valuable feedback about their current state. Once obtained you can then take this information and apply your understanding of ***human movement science,*** to implement the ***training principles*** in a program specifically designed to meet your client's Goals, Needs, and Abilities.

It's a fundamental understanding of each of these areas that allow trainers to design effective programs. It's not enough to apply only one aspect such as training principles. We must also understand the human body and human movement science. Think of a mechanic who works on a car. They have to understand the parts of the vehicle and their function in order to diagnose and fix any issues that arise.

It's the same with understanding and addressing issues with the human body. If a client's feet turn out and knees cave in during a squat assessment, we wouldn't have them doing calf raises and adduction exercises initially, as those muscles are suspected to be overactive with that compensation. Strengthening them could make the compensation worse. We would take care of those muscular imbalances first by lengthening the tight muscles *(calves and adductors)* while strengthening the opposing weaker muscles involved in abduction.

Be aware that when a client initially starts a training program, they are likely to be in a **deconditioned state**. They could have *muscle imbalances, decreased flexibility, or lack of core and joint stability.* Remember the saying ***"Straighten the body before you Strengthen it."*** You want to get the client stable and aligned before loading their movement. If the training intensity is too high initially or you *load faulty movement patterns* the client could experience excessive overload which **may lead to injury.**

Assessments are used to get a *baseline* of your client's *current fitness level* which can then be used as a trackable indicator for the goals they have set. Reassessments can show valuable progress that helps clients to continue towards their goal or make adjustments along the way. Remember to always use the *client-centered approach* thinking of yourself more as a *coach or mentor* to provide solutions and focus on positive outcomes. It is especially important in the beginning to ensure your clients have *positive experiences* with exercise and look forward to the next training session with you. As your clients gain confidence in their exercise abilities, further assessments can be made and the training volume and/or intensity can be progressively increased. Show your clients how it applies to them in a meaningful way.

Sequence of Assessments

Initial needs assessments should begin with reviewing a client's health history, completing the intake forms and questionnaires, discussing desires, preferences, general goals, and then determining which assessments are relevant and a timeline to conduct them. Periodic reassessments are important to gauge a client's progress towards goal achievement.

1) **Health-risk appraisal**

2) **Resting vital signs**: Heart rate and blood pressure

3) **Body Composition**: Height, Weight, Body Mass Index (BMI), Waist to Hip Ratio (WHR), Skinfold measurements *Quarterly body composition assessments are appropriate.*

4) **Static posture and movement screens**

5) **Joint flexibility and muscle length**: Sit-and-reach test

6) **Balance and core function**: Static and dynamic

7) **Cardiovascular Fitness**: Cycle ergometer tests; Ventilatory threshold testing; Field test *(Rockport fitness 1-mile walking test, 1.5-mile run test);* Step tests *(YMCA submaximal step test)*

8) **Muscular Fitness**: Muscular endurance *(Push-up test, Curl-up test, Body-weight squat test)* Muscular strength *(1-RM testing for bench-press, leg-press and squat, Submaximal strength test)*

9) **Skill-related assessments**: Balance, Agility, Coordination, Reaction time, Speed, and Power.

Sample assessment sequencing can be found in Table 7-1 on page 221 of the Exercise Professional's Guide to Personal Training.

Personal trainers must always be aware of *signs or symptoms that merit immediate test termination* when conducting any exercise test involving exertion with their clients and refer them to a qualified healthcare professional if necessary. Signs of serious health issues may not be present until the client exerts themselves. These signs and symptoms include the following:

- Onset of angina, chest pain, or angina-like symptoms
- Significant drop (>10 mmHg) in systolic blood pressure (SBP) despite an increase in exercise intensity
- Excessive rise in blood pressure (BP): SBP reaches >250 mmHg, or diastolic blood pressure (DBP) reaches >115 mmHg
- Excess fatigue, shortness of breath, or wheezing *(does not include heavy breathing due to intense exercise)*
- Signs of poor perfusion: lightheadedness, pallor *(pale skin)*, cyanosis *(bluish coloration, especially around the mouth)*, nausea, or cold and clammy skin
- Increase nervous system symptoms *(e.g., ataxia, dizziness, confusion, or syncope)*
- Leg cramping or claudication
- Client request to stop
- Physical or verbal manifestations of severe fatigue
- Failure of testing equipment

Objective Assessments

Heart Rate Sites

1) Radial artery *(thumb side of the wrist)*
2) Brachial artery *(anterior side of the elbow)*
3) Carotid artery *(neck)*

The *carotid artery is not the preferred site* due to the possibility of reflexive slowing of the heart rate when pressed. *Radial and brachial are the locations of choice.*

Body Composition: The relative proportion of lean tissue to body-fat tissue in the body.
*A certain amount of **essential body fat** is necessary, for men it's between 2 and 5%, and for women, it is between 10 and 13%.*

Lean Body Weight (LBW): The amount of fat-free weight (mass) one has.

Desired Body Weight (DBW) = Lean body weight ÷ (100% - Desired body fat %)

Body Fat Distribution: The location of fat on the body.

Waist to Hip ratio is a good indicator of body fat distribution. Waist ÷ Hip = WHR

Basal Metabolic Rate (BMR): Calories burned daily without movement.

To gain or lose weight one should increase or decrease calories by 300 to 400 kcals per day.

Height and Weight Conversions

- 1" = 2.54 cm
- 1 m = 100 cm
- 1 Kg = 2.2 pounds

Body Mass Index (BMI): A weight to height ratio / *BMI = Weight (Kg) ÷ Height (m²)*

BMI cannot determine actual body composition, which means it can unfairly categorize some individuals *(someone with a lot of muscle mass could be put in the "obese" category)*

Waist to Hip Ratio (WHR) Waist circumference ÷ Hip circumference = Waist to Hip ratio

- Health risk is high when above 0.95 for men and 0.86 for women
- Health risk is high when waist circumference is ≥39.5" for men and ≥35.5" for women
- Low risk is ≤31.5" for men and ≤27.5" for women

See Table 7-7 on Page 241 of the Exercise Professional's Guide to Personal Training

Skinfold Measurement Jackson and Pollock 3-site locations to determine body fat percentage

- Chest, Thigh, and Abdomen for men
- Triceps, Thigh, and Suprailium for women

Skill related assessment considerations: The Pro agility test and 40-yard dash are both appropriate assessments for speed, agility, and quickness testing. These tests along with power assessments *(Standing long jump test and Vertical jump test)* are designed for clients interested in performance training. The majority of normative data presented with these tests has been obtained from studies involving athletes. Little if any data exists for middle-aged or older adults. The results of these tests are best utilized as baseline data against which to measure a client's future performance. Keep in mind the majority of clients will not progress to this performance stage of training.

Muscular Fitness testing considerations: Submaximal strength testing can be used with a high amount of accuracy to determine a client's likely **one-repetition maximum (1-RM)**. 1-RM testing should only be performed during the Load / Speed phase of the ACE IFT Model due to a certain amount of risk involved with maximal exertion.

Cardiorespiratory Fitness (CRF): A person's ability to perform large muscle movements over a sustained period; related to the capacity of the heart-lung system to deliver oxygen for sustained energy production *(Also called cardiorespiratory endurance or aerobic fitness)*.

Posture and Movement Term Definitions

Posture: The arrangement of the body and its limbs.

Static Posture: The alignment of the body's segments, how the person holds themselves *"statically"* with no movement in space. This is a good starting point to identify potential muscular imbalances and potential movement compensations associated with poor posture.

Dynamic Posture: The position the body is in at any moment during a movement pattern.

Balance: The ability to maintain the body's position over its *Base of Support (BOS)* within stability limits, both statically and dynamically.

Static Balance: The ability to maintain the body's *Center of Gravity (COG)* within its Base of Support (BOS)

Dynamic Balance: The act of maintaining postural control while moving.

Static Posture Assessments

Postural Deviations are examples of poor static or dynamic posture. They are predictable patterns of muscular imbalances that can lead to decreased neuromuscular efficiency and tissue overload. *Lordosis, Kyphosis, Flat back, Sway back, and Scoliosis.*

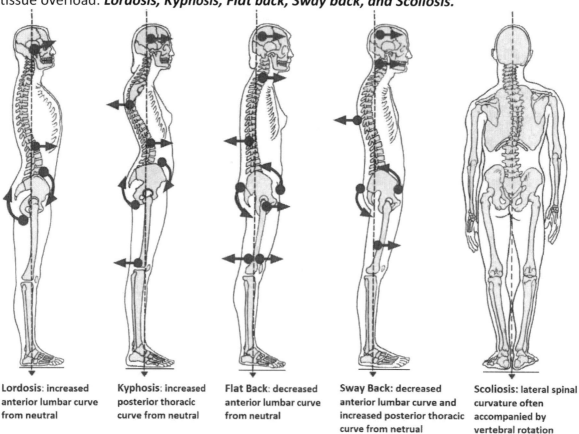

Lordosis: increased anterior lumbar curve from neutral

Kyphosis: increased posterior thoracic curve from neutral

Flat Back: decreased anterior lumbar curve from neutral

Sway Back: decreased anterior lumbar curve and increased posterior thoracic curve from netrual

Scoliosis: lateral spinal curvature often accompanied by vertebral rotation

The muscular imbalances associated with these deviations can be found in Tables 10-1 thru 10-4 on pages 394 and 395 of the Exercise Professional's Guide to Personal Training.

5 Common Compensations occur along the 5 kinetic chain checkpoints:

> ➤ **Subtalar pronation (Ankle)** *(feet turn out)* / **Supination** *(feet turn inward)*

> ➤ **Hip Adduction** *(One hip higher than the other "hip hiking")*

> ➤ **Pelvic Tilting** *(Lordosis / Flat back)*

> ➤ **Shoulder Position and Thoracic Spine** *(Kyphosis)*

> ➤ **Head Position** *(Forward head / See Table 10-9 Page 406)*

*Figure 10-18 from pages 407 – 409 of the Exercise Professional's Guide to Personal Training. gives a sample postural assessment checklist.

When observing static posture look for alignment of the **5-Kinetic Chain Checkpoints**. Starting from the ground up at the **Ankle, Knee, Hip, Shoulder, and Head.** Posture will be assessed from the front, back, and side views. Trainers should focus on the larger more obvious imbalances and avoid noting minor postural asymmetries.

Postural deviations and muscle imbalance can be attributed to many correctible and non-correctible factors.

> ➤ **Correctible factors**:
>> o Repetitive movements *(muscular pattern overload)*
>> o Awkward positions and movements *(habitually poor posture)*
>> o Side dominance
>> o Lack of joint stability and mobility
>> o Imbalanced strength-training programs

> ➤ **Non-correctible factors**:
>> o Congenital conditions *(scoliosis)*
>> o Some pathologies *(arthritis)*
>> o Structural deviations
>> o Certain types of trauma *(surgery, injury, or amputation)*

The First Step to understanding muscular imbalances is to learn the major muscles of the body *(prime movers)* and their functions *(reference the anatomy websites on our resources blog)*. **To remember a muscle's function visualize what happens when the muscle contracts.** *Biceps contract to flex the elbow joint / Triceps contract to extend the elbow joint.*

The Next Step is to practice by taking yourself, friends, or family members through the same process that you will take a client through. First stand with good static posture aligning the kinetic chain checkpoints **(feet, knees, hips, shoulders, head).** Then put yourself in each of the deviated positions **(Lordosis, Kyphosis, Sway back, Flat back).** Visualize the **Tug-of-War** going on with the muscles and which ones are winning. **Hip flexors and Erector spinae are "winning" in the Lordosis position causing an Anterior / front pelvic tilt.*

Movement Assessments are covered from *pages 429 – 440 of the Exercise Professional's Guide to Personal Training.* You will be checking the 5-kinetic chain checkpoints through most of these assessments from both front and side views.

> **Bend-and-Lift** *(Squat mechanics)* Tibia and Torso should be parallel to each other.

> **Single-Leg Step-up** *(Isolate each leg to check for imbalance)*

> **Push Assessment** *(Shoulder push stabilization)* Scapular winging, collapsing of the core.

> **Pull Assessment** *(Standing Row / Shoulder and scapula function) Common* compensations include shoulders elevating or rounding forward in protraction (kyphosis), the head moving forward, lumbar spine hyperextending (rounding) lordosis

> **Rotation Assessment** *(Thoracic spine mobility)* Hold a dowel in a seated position with arms crossed and rotate to measure the degree of rotation.

Balance Assessment protocols are listed from *pages 410 thru 413 of the Exercise Professional's Guide to Personal Training.*

> **Static Balance**: Unipedal Stance Test *(stand on dominant leg eyes open or closed / Table 10-10 on page 411 gives the normative times for test.)*

> **Dynamic Balance**: Y Balance Test *(Figure 10-23 Page 412 shows the layout)*

Muscular Endurance assessments are listed from *pages 413 thru 419 of the Exercise Professional's Guide to Personal Training.*

> **McGill's Torso Muscular Endurance Test Battery**: Trunk flexor *(top of sit up)*, Trunk lateral endurance *(side plank),* trunk extensor *(roman chair / table)*

The following are the recommended ratios of hold times between the test protocols.

> Flexion / extension ratio should be less than 1.0
> Right-side bridge / Left-side bridge should be no greater than 0.05 from a balanced score of 1.0
> Side bridge / extension ratio should be less than 0.75

Flexibility Assessments are shown from *pages 420 – 428 of the Exercise Professional's Guide to Personal Training.* Figures 10-33 - 10-35 show the normal joint range of motion for various limbs and positions. You do not have to memorize these angles but it's a great reference if you come across a client with limited movement and muscular imbalances.

> **Thomas Test** *(Hip Flexor / Quadriceps Length)*

> **Passive Straight-leg Raise**

> **Shoulder Flexion and Extension**

Muscular Strength Assessments are covered from *pages 446 – 456 of the Exercise Professional's Guide to Personal Training.* Strength can be expressed as either *absolute strength* or *relative strength.* Absolute strength is the greatest amount of weight that can be lifted one time and is defined as a *one-repetition maximum 1RM.* Relative strength takes the person's body weight into account and is used when comparing individuals. You take 1RM / Bodyweight.

> **1-RM Bench-Press** *(Upper body strength)*

> **1-RM Squat Assessment** *(Lower body strength)*

Submaximal Strength Assessments can also be used. These are often more practical and safer to use with inexperienced exercisers, or for individuals with health considerations where a 1RM test would be contraindicated. *Table 10-27 on page 456 of the Exercise Professional's Guide to Personal Training* gives 1RM prediction coefficients for both Squat and Bench movements. The chart below shows the percentage of 1RM based on reps performed.

* 225 x 4 reps (225 ÷ 0.90) = 250 lb 1RM

Repetitions	% of 1RM
1	100%
2	95%
3	93%
4	90%
5	87%
6	85%
7	83%
8	80%
9	77%
10	75%
11	70%
12	67%
15	65%

Power Assessments are covered from *pages 456 – 459 of the Exercise Professional's Guide to Personal Training.* Power is generally sport or activity specific so power assessments are only necessary for those with power related goals, such as increasing vertical jump height. Those with special considerations, injuries, or orthopedic issues should not perform power assessments.

> **Vertical Jump** *(Lower extremity power)*

Speed, Agility, and Quickness Assessments are covered from *pages 459 – 460 of the Exercise Professional's Guide to Personal Training.*

> **T-Test** *(Multidirectional movement ability)*

Stability and Mobility points of the Kinetic Chain

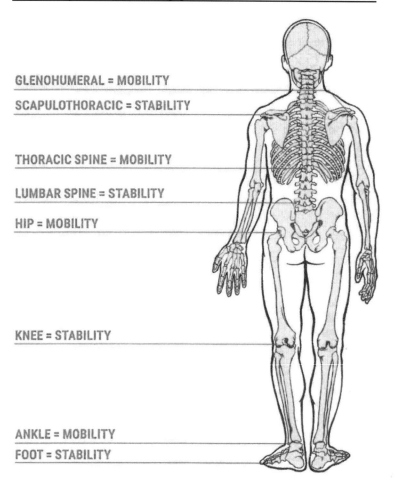

GLENOHUMERAL = MOBILITY

SCAPULOTHORACIC = STABILITY

THORACIC SPINE = MOBILITY

LUMBAR SPINE = STABILITY

HIP = MOBILITY

KNEE = STABILITY

ANKLE = MOBILITY

FOOT = STABILITY

The kinetic chain should be viewed as an actual chain, everything is connected. It's helpful to think of a ***ground-up approach*** to addressing issues *(fixing issues with the foot before the knee, or thoracic spine and shoulder before the head and neck).* You can also think of fixing issues that are ***more proximal (closer to the core) before fixing distal issues.*** Oftentimes the source of pain and/or imbalance comes from further upstream or downstream in the kinetic chain.

A herniated disc in the lumbar spine can cause sciatica in the hip and nerve pain in the legs, even though the cause in the lower back. Physical Therapists refer to ***centralizing the pain***, as the disc herniation improves the pain will move from the legs closer to the source in the lower back.

Another example is knee valgus *(knees caving inward).* This is often caused by the feet turning outward, which can be caused by a tight piriformis in the hip. The causes and correlations can come from both upstream and downstream the kinetic chain.

Anatomy and Kinesiology

Kinesiology is the study of the mechanics of human movement and specifically evaluates muscles, joints, and skeletal structures and their involvement in movement.

- **Biomechanics**: The study of how forces affect a living body. Evaluation of how the body moves.
- **Musculoskeletal anatomy**
- **Neuromuscular physiology**

Definitions of Anatomical Locations and Positions

Anterior: Toward or on the front side of the body.

Posterior: Toward or on the back side of the body.

Superior: Toward the head; *higher*

Inferior: Away from the head; *lower*

Proximal: Toward the center of the body or nearest to the center from a point of reference.

Distal: Away from the center of the body or point of reference.

Medial: Toward the midline of the body

Lateral: Away from the midline of the body; to the side

Contralateral: Body part located on the opposite side of the body. *(right hand / left foot)*

Ipsilateral: Body part located on the same side of the body. *(right hand / right foot)*

Anatomical position: Standard posture wherein the body stands upright with the arms beside the trunk, the palms face forward, and the head faces forward.

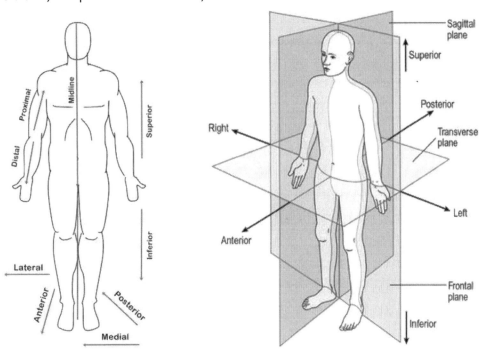

Planes and Axes of Motion

- **Sagittal plane**: Divides the body into the right and left sides. *Flexion and extension* exercises are primarily involved in this plane, also *dorsiflexion, and plantar flexion. *Squats, bicep curls, walking, and running are examples of Sagittal plane movements.*

- **Frontal plane**: Divides the body into anterior and posterior (front / back) portions. Vertical and lateral movements occur in this plane: *abduction and adduction, lateral flexion at the spine, and eversion and inversion of the foot. *Jumping jacks, side lunges, lateral raises, and windmills are examples of Frontal plane movements.*

- **Transverse plane**: Divides the body into superior and inferior (top / bottom) portions. Horizontal and rotational movements take place in the transverse plane: *internal and external rotation, pronation and supination, horizontal abduction and adduction. *Trunk rotation and swinging a bat or horizontal abduction and adduction are examples of Transverse plane movements.*

- **Medial-lateral axis**: Straight line that cuts through the body laterally side to side. In the sagittal plane, rotation happens around this axis. *A hip hinge is a movement that occurs around a medial-lateral axis.*

- **Anterior-posterior axis**: Straight line that cuts through the body from front to back. In the frontal plane, rotation happens around this axis. *Raising an arm laterally is a movement that occurs* around an anterior-posterior axis.

- **Longitudinal axis**: Straight line that cuts through the body from top to bottom. Rotation around a longitudinal axis takes place in the transverse plane. *Spinal rotation with twisting of the trunk is an example of a movement around a longitudinal axis.*

The plane in which an exercise occurs is in relation to the body not the position of the body. *Performing jumping jacks while standing up and making a snow angel while lying on the ground are both frontal plane movements.*

It helps to visualize the planes and know which movements occur in each. *A visual representation of the planes can be found in Figure 9-5 on page 328 of the Exercise Professional's Guide to Personal Training.*

There is also a great video that explains the planes of motion that was put out by the *Brookbrush Institute.* This video is linked in our personal trainer resources blog. **www.cptprep.com/single-post/resources**

Movement Term Definitions

Supine Position: Lying face up.

Prone Position: Lying face down.

Flexion: Movement involving a decrease in joint angle. ***Bending movement (towards, closer)*** A bicep curl involves elbow flexion with the lower arm moving closer to the upper arm and ending with the hand by the shoulder. The bottom of a squat is another example. The ankle, knee, and hip joints are in flexion.

Extension: Movement involving an increase in joint angle. ***Straightening movement (extended, away, further)*** The lowering of a biceps curl extends the elbow joint, and the lifting portion of a deadlift extends both the knee and hip joints.

Adduction: Movement toward the midline of the body, usually in the frontal plane.
* Think Adding together, Adduction starts with word "Add"

Abduction: Movement away from the midline of the body, usually in the frontal plane.

Plantar flexion: Movement at the ankle joint that points the foot downward.
* Like a ballerina

Dorsiflexion: Movement at the ankle joint that points the foot up towards the leg.
* Like a dorsal fin. The ability to dorsiflex the ankle is key for proper squat mechanics.

Inversion: Movement of the foot which causes the sole of the foot to face inwards. When someone rolls their ankle during sports this is typically an extreme inversion of the foot. You can also picture someone who walks bow-legged or pigeon-toed.

Eversion: Movement of the foot which causes the sole of the foot to face outwards. The foot would move into eversion when someone's knees cave in during a low squat. Their feet will turn out and away.

Supination of the foot: A combination of plantar flexion, inversion, and adduction.

Pronation of the foot: A combination of dorsiflexion, eversion, and abduction.

Rotation: Right or left twist in the transverse plane, usually used to describe neck and trunk movement.
- **Internal Rotation**: Rotation of a joint toward the middle of the body.
- **External Rotation**: Rotation of a joint away from the middle of the body.

Circumduction: A compound circular movement involving flexion, extension, abduction, and adduction, circumscribing a cone shape. The shoulder and hip are capable of circumduction, arm circles.

*The Exercise Professionals Guide gives a visual for all of these various types of movements starting in Figure 9.6 on page 329 and continuing thru figure 9.9 on page 333.

Types of Movements

Open chain movements occur when a distal segment *(hand or foot)* moves in space.

- *Bicep Curls, triceps extensions, Leg extensions, and Leg curls are examples of open chain movements.*

Closed chain movements occur when distal segments are fixed in place.

- *Push-ups, Pull-ups, Squats, Deadlift, and Lunges are examples of closed chain movements.*

Range of Motion (ROM) is the amount of movement produced by one or more joints.

Center of Gravity (COG) in the human body is generally at the level of the second sacral vertebra, but it varies from person to person and changes with body position.

Figure 9-29 on page 358 of the Exercise Professional's Guide to Personal Training shows some positional examples.

Gravity pulls on the body in a straight line through its center of gravity. This is known as *line of gravity* or line of pull. To maintain balance without moving a person's line of gravity must fall within their *Base of Support (BOS).* These are the points of the body in contact with the ground. BOS is usually the space between our feet but it can also involve other parts of our body in different positions such as a 3-point stance used in football or at the start of a sprint.

Multijoint movements involve using two or more joints to perform the movement.

Multiplanar movements occur in more than one plane of motion.

Incorporating functional exercises that include both multijoint and multiplanar movements that mimic activities of daily living will set clients up for long-term success.

Movements of the Scapula

Elevation: Movement of the scapula superiorly *(upwards)* in the frontal plane.

Depression: Movement of the scapula inferiorly *(downwards)* in the frontal plane.

Retraction (adduction): Movement of the scapula toward the spine in the frontal plane. *Inward, Shoulders move back, and chest moves up and out.*

Protraction (abduction): Movement of the scapula away from the spine in the frontal plane. *Outward, Rounded shoulders. *Associated with Kyphosis postural deviation.*

Upward rotation: Superior and lateral movement of the inferior angle of the scapula in the frontal plane.

Downward rotation: Inferior and medial movement of the inferior angle of the scapula in the frontal plane.

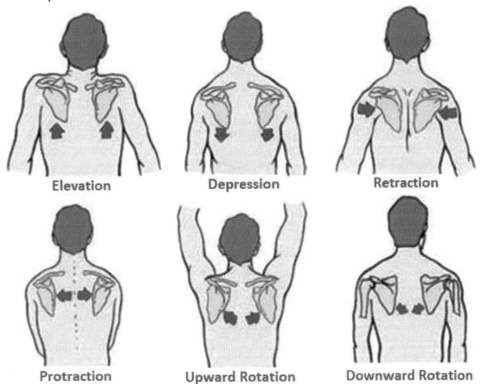

There is a short *1-minute video showing all of the muscles involved with each movement of the scapula* linked on our Personal Trainer Resources blog. **www.cptprep.com/single-post/resources**

Pages 403 – 405 of the Exercise Professional's Guide to Personal Training go over common shoulder positions and deviations along with the suspected overactive tight muscles for each deviation.

Typically, the muscles involved in *retraction* and *depression* are going to be *underactive* with most deviations.

The Human Movement System is comprised of (3) interwoven systems that allow our bodies to move.

The *Skeletal System* is the foundation and gives structure through our kinetic chain of joints.
The *Nervous System* is the communication network within the human body.
The *Muscular System* is the motor that drives our bodies to move.

The Skeletal System

The skeletal system is the body's framework, composed of bones and joints. **The skeletal system serves the following (5) major roles in the body**:

- *Movement*: The skeletal system consists of levers *(bones)* and pivot points *(joints)* the muscular system acts upon to create movement.
- *Support*: Bones are the framework of the body that everything else is built on top of or held within.
- *Protection*: Bones encase vital organs and protect them from trauma. The skull protects the brain, and the rib cage protects the heart and lungs.
- *Blood production*: Blood cells are formed in the bone marrow which is housed in the cavity of certain bones in the body.
- *Mineral storage*: Minerals such as calcium and phosphorus are stored in bones.

Similar to the nervous system the skeletal system is composed of two main systems.

- **Axial Skeleton** is made up of the skull, sternum, rib cage, and vertebral column. *Composed of 80 bones* This system correlates with the area of the **Central Nervous System** (brain and spinal cord)

- **Appendicular Skeleton** is made of the upper and lower extremities as well as the shoulder and pelvic girdles. *Composed of 126 bones* This system correlates with the **Peripheral Nervous System.**

The bones of the skeletal system are categorized into (5) major categories: Long bones, short bones, flat bones, irregular bones, and sesamoid bones.

Long bones are characterized by their long cylindrical shaft with irregular or widen ends. The *humerus* of the upper arm *(surrounded by bicep / triceps)* and *femur* of the upper leg *(surrounded by quads / hamstrings)* are examples of long bones. They are composed of 3 parts.

- *Epiphysis*: The end of the long bone, the primary site for bone growth, involved in red blood cell production. *Epiphysis starts with "E" so it's the End of the bone.* This would be the area towards the hip or knee for the femur

- *Diaphysis*: The shaft portion of a long bone and is mainly comprised of compact bone.

- *Epiphyseal plates* connect the two portions of the bone and where growth takes place.

Bones are living tissues in the body that adapt and become stronger with weight-bearing exercise which increases *bone density, mass, and strength.* This is why strength training is important for older individuals *(as our bone mass peaks around age 35).* In order to keep strong bones, we must load our system.

Older individuals are at a higher risk of hip fracture because bones tend to weaken with age (known as osteoporosis). Balance problems also make older people more likely to trip and fall, which is one of the most common causes of hip fracture. Leg strength, balance, and bone density are all beneficial to maintain into old age to help mitigate some of the common injuries in the older population.

Vertebral Column

The vertebral column *(backbone or spine)* consists of a series of irregularly shaped bones called vertebrae. There are 24 individual vertebrae in the spine:

- 7 Cervical (support the head and neck)
- 12 Thoracic (Mid-back) *Ribs are connected to these*
- 5 Lumbar (Low-back, supports most of the weight of the body)

We eat breakfast at 7, lunch at 12, and dinner at 5 is a good way to remember the vertebrae.

There are also fused vertebrae located in the sacrum *(Tailbone).*

There are natural curves of the spine that include: *Cervical, Thoracic, Lumbar, and Sacral*

The optimal arrangement of these curves is called neutral spine which is a position of good posture where the vertebrae and associated structures are under the least amount of load.

- Kyphosis: Primary curves *(thoracic / sacral) *rounding forward*
- Lordosis: Secondary curves *(cervical / lumbar) *rounding backward*
- Hyperkyphosis or Hyperlordosis: Deviations of the spine in the sagittal plane
- Scoliosis: Lateral deviation of the spine in the frontal plane.

Figure 9-3 on page 326 of the Exercise Professional's Guide to Personal Training shows a diagram of the vertebral column.

Types of Joints

Joints are the sites in the body where movement occurs as the result of a muscle contraction. Joints form junctions between bones that are connected by muscles and connective tissue.
The muscles pull on our bones and connective tissue to cause movement around a joint.
The three main types of joints are *fibrous, cartilaginous, and synovial.*

Fibrous and Cartilaginous (Non-synovial) joints are held together by connective tissue and allow little or no movement. *Found in sutures of the skull and the joint between the ends of the tibia and fibula in the lower leg.*

Synovial joints: Joints that are held together by a joint capsule and ligaments; they are most associated with movement in the body. Four general movements occur in synovial joints: *Gliding, Angular, Circumduction, and Rotation.*
Synovial joints comprise 80% of all joints in the body.

Types of Synovial joints: Hinge, gliding, condyloid, saddle, pivot, and ball-and-socket.

> ➤ **Hinge joints** are formed between two or more bones where the bones can only move along one axis to flex or extend. *Ankle and Elbow joints are examples of hinge joints.*

> ➤ **Ball-and-Socket** is a type of synovial joint where the ball-shaped surface of one bone fits into a cup-like depression of another bone. These joints are capable of moving on multiple axes from the common center of the ball joint. *Hip and Shoulder joints are examples of ball and socket joints.*

Arthrokinematics: The motions of the joints in the body.
The three major motions are Roll, Slide, and Spin.

Arthrokinematic Dysfunction *(altered joint motion)*: Caused by altered length-tension relationships and force-couple relationships that affect the joints and leads to abnormal joint movement *(arthrokinematics)* and proprioception causing poor movement efficiency.

Connective Tissue

➤ **Tendons** are tough, cord-like tissues that connect *muscles to bones.*

➤ **Ligaments** are tough, flexible fibrous connective tissue that connects *bone to bone.*

➤ **Fasciae** is a band or sheet of connective tissue beneath the skin that attaches, stabilizes, encloses, and separates muscles and other internal organs.

Joints are surrounded by these connective tissues.

Tendons link muscle to bone / Ligaments link bone to bone.

Tendons and ligaments have a low blood supply which is why they are slower to heal from injury and take longer to adapt to exercise-induced stresses, compared to muscles.

Collagen is the most abundant protein in the body. Collagen fibers provide stability and structure due to their tensile strength and inextensibility properties. They control and limit excessive movement of our joints through our connective tissue of tendons and ligaments.

Elastin is another key protein. It is highly elastic and present in connective tissue allowing many tissues in the body to *resume their shape* after stretching or contracting. These elastic fibers are what help our skin *return to its original resting state* after it is poked or pinched.

Elastic fibers are almost always found together with collagen fibers. They work together to support and facilitate joint movement.

The Nervous System

The nervous system gives and receives inputs that tell our bodies when to move, in which direction, and at what speed. Think of the nervous system as the *software* and the muscular and skeletal systems as the *hardware.* *Another way is to think of the nervous system as the *conductor* and the muscles as the *orchestra*.

Neuron: The functional unit of the nervous system. A specialized cell that processes and transmits information through both electrical and chemical signals.

The (3) primary functions of the nervous system are *sensory (input), integrative (analyze input), and motor function (response)* There are 3 classifications of neurons that correspond to each.

➢ **Sensory function:** The ability of the nervous system to sense changes in either our *internal* or *external* environment. **(Sensory) Afferent neurons** respond to touch, sounds, light, and other stimuli and they transmit this information back to the brain.

➢ **Integrative function:** The ability of the nervous system to analyze and interpret sensory information to allow for proper decision making, which produces the appropriate response. *Interneurons* transmit information from one neuron to another.

➢ **Motor function**: The neuromuscular response to the sensory information. **(Motor) Efferent neurons** send the signal back from the brain and spinal cord to the muscles.

Cognitive example: Someone asks you a question *(sensory input),* you *analyze* and think about what they said and then you formulate a *response*.

Physical example: You touch something that is hot, the sensory input sends the signal back to your brain *(integrative function),* and your brain then sends a signal down to your muscles to pull your hand away from the hot object.

➢ *Afferent neurons go towards the brain (incoming information)*
➢ *Efferent neurons go away from the brain (outgoing response to stimuli)*

Neural activation is the communication link between the nervous system and the muscular system. It describes the contraction of a muscle generated by neural stimulation. This happens at the **motor unit** which is the point at which the motor neuron meets the muscle fibers it activates.

Neurotransmitters are chemical messengers that cross the *neuromuscular junction (synapse)* to transmit electrical impulses from the nerve to the muscle.

Central Nervous System (CNS): The division of the nervous system comprising the brain and the spinal cord. Its primary function is to coordinate the activity of all parts of the body.

Peripheral Nervous System (PNS): The portion of the nervous system that is outside the brain and spinal cord. The primary function is to connect the central nervous system (CNS) to the limbs and organs, serving as a communication relay with the rest of the body.

> **Somatic Nervous System (SNS)** responsible for voluntary muscle contraction or movement.

> **Autonomic Nervous System (ANS)**: The part of the nervous system responsible for the control of the bodily functions *not consciously directed*, such as breathing, the heartbeat, and digestive processes.

>> o **Sympathetic Nervous System (SNS)**: Part of the autonomic nervous system (ANS) that activates what is often termed the *"fight or flight"* response. The sympathetic nervous system is activated when there is a stressor or emergency, such as severe pain, anger, or fear.

>> o **Parasympathetic Nervous System (PNS)**: Part of the autonomic nervous system (ANS) that stimulates *"rest and digestion"* physiological processes.

Breathing is one example that is *autonomic* the majority of the time *(we are not consciously thinking about it, this is why we still breathe when we are sleeping)*. However, we can also *consciously control our breath*. This is one extremely valuable and readily available way that we can control our nervous system response to stressors. If a stressor causes an overly sympathetic fight or flight response, we can take slow controlled breaths through our nose with *longer exhales to downregulate towards a more parasympathetic state.* We can also use our breath to downregulate from a hard workout or to deal with daily life stressors that we all have. Breathing techniques *(longer inhale, shorter exhale)* can also be used to ramp up mental alertness for a competition or presentation by increasing our sympathetic activity. Performance is generally best when we are somewhere in the middle of parasympathetic and sympathetic. *We want to be alert enough to perform but calm enough to focus.*

The Arousal Continuum

Panic
Very Stressed
Stressed
Highly Alert
Alert & Calm
Alert
Drowsy
Deep Sleep
Coma

Parasympathetic Nervous System

Sympathetic Nervous System

Our stress response *"fight or flight system"* is not always bad, it is there for a reason. It's a valuable tool that allows our body to respond and take action when necessary. However, if our system is chronically elevated in a state of stress or anxiety it can become problematic.

Proprioception

Proprioception describes the cumulative sensory input to the central nervous system from all mechanoreceptors that sense body position and limb movements. Think of proprioception as *awareness*, our central nervous systems *(brain)* ability to talk to our muscles *(body)*. It's knowing where the body is in relation to its various segments and the external environment.

In order to have good proprioception, we must have *optimal length-tension, force-couple relationships, and joint function.* Kinetic chain imbalances can alter balance and cause neuromuscular inefficiency. *Like a kink in a garden hose, once it has a kink the water flows more slowly or not at all.* Imbalances and injuries are like a kink in our system, and they inhibit our ability to activate and control our muscles synergistically. Flawed movement patterns can also alter the firing order of the muscles activated, which alters movement patterns and decreases neuromuscular efficiency.

Proprioceptors are specialized sensory receptors located within joints, muscles, and tendons that provide the central nervous system with information needed to maintain muscle tone and perform complex coordinated movements.

Mechanoreceptors: Sensory receptors responsible for sensing pressure and distortion in body tissues. *These primarily pertain to human movement.*

> - **Muscle spindles** sense any stretching or tension within a muscle; their primary function is to respond to the stretch of a muscle and through a reflex action initiate a stronger muscle action *(contraction)* to reduce the stretch. This is called the *"Stretch reflex."* * Muscle spindles prevent overstretching and potential muscular damage.*

> - **Golgi tendon organs (GTO)** attach to the tendons near the junction of the muscle. GTO's detect differences in tension and when excessive tension is detected they send a signal to relax the muscle to prevent injury resulting from over-contraction *(autogenic inhibition)* GTO will signal the muscle to relax after approximately 10 seconds of applied tension to the muscle.

> - **Joint receptors**: Receptors in and around a joint that respond to pressure, acceleration, and deceleration of the joint.

Think of the *Muscle spindles* and *Golgi tendon organs* like they are in a *Tug-of-War* with each other. *Muscle spindles (contract)* ⟷ *Golgi tendon organs (relax).*

The Muscular System

There are (3) types of muscle: *Skeletal, Cardiac, and Smooth*

Skeletal muscles are consciously controlled. They provide locomotion and stability to the skeletal system. There are more than 600 skeletal muscles in the human body. Approximately 100 are primary movement muscles. These are the focus of the personal trainer to help clients achieve increased skeletal muscle activation, coordination, strength, size *(hypertrophy)*, and form during movement patterns.

Muscle Fiber Types: Type I *(slow-twitch)*, Type IIx *(fast-twitch)*, Type IIa *(intermediate)*
*Type IIa is a hybrid with both fast-twitch (explosive) and slow-twitch (endurance) capabilities.

Type I Characteristics: Red in color, smaller in size, produce less force, slow to fatigue, higher aerobic capacity due to a large number of capillaries, mitochondria, and myoglobin for increased oxygen delivery and usage.

Muscles that act primarily as stabilizers generally contain greater concentrations of *Type I (slow-twitch, endurance)* muscle fibers. The core muscles are an example of this as they stabilize the spine during loading and movement throughout the day. Stabilizer muscles are better suited for endurance-type training *(higher-volume, lower-intensity)*.

Type II Characteristics: White in color, larger in size, produce more force, quick to fatigue, higher anaerobic capacity, and decreased oxygen delivery due to fewer capillaries, mitochondria, and myoglobin.

Muscles primarily responsible for joint movement generally contain greater concentrations of *Type II (fast-twitch, explosive)* muscle fibers. These muscles are better suited for strength and power-type training *(higher-intensity, lower-volume)*.

*All muscles have a combination of slow and fast-twitch fibers that will vary depending on the function of the muscle.

Muscle has the following (4) behavioral properties:

- *Extensibility*: The ability to be stretched or lengthened.

- *Elasticity*: The ability to return to normal or resting length after being stretched.

- *Irritability*: The ability to respond to a stimulus.

- *Ability to develop tension*

Structure of Skeletal Muscle

- **Epimysium**: The outermost layer of the muscle, made up of connective tissue that lies underneath the fascia and surrounds the muscle.
- **Perimysium**: Connective tissue that wraps around bundles of muscle fibers *(fascicles)*.
- **Endomysium**: The innermost layer of connective tissue that surrounds the individual muscle fibers.

The smallest contractile unit of a muscle fiber *(cell)* is called a **Sarcomere**. Sarcomeres are made up of two types of muscle protein: **Actin** *(thin filament)* and **Myosin** *(thick filament)* which slide across each other to provide muscle contraction *(sliding filament theory).* The arrangement of myosin and actin gives the skeletal muscle its striated appearance.

Sliding-Filament Theory states that actin filaments at each end of the sarcomere slide inward on myosin filaments, pulling the Z-lines toward the center of the sarcomere and thus shortening the muscle fiber.

Underactive Muscle

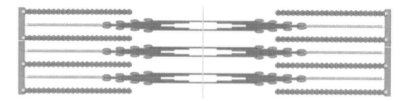

Optimal Length Tension Relationship

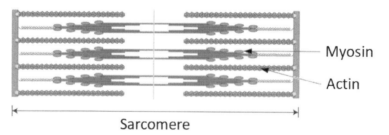

Myosin

Actin

Sarcomere

Overactive Muscle

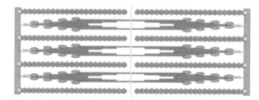

The number of cross-bridges that are formed between actin and myosin at any instant in time dictates the force production of a muscle. Muscle force capability is greatest when the muscle is at its resting length due to the increased opportunity for actin-myosin cross-bridges. If a muscle is contracted or stretched the force capability is reduced.

Muscle Alignment and Neural Activation

Length-Tension Relationship (LTR): The resting length of a muscle and the tension the muscle can produce at that resting length. LTR describes the relationship between the contractile proteins *(actin and myosin)* of a sarcomere and their force-generating capacity. When these contractile proteins are ideally aligned with the most cross-bridging they can produce the greatest amount of force. Shortening or lengthening minimizes the cross-bridges reducing the muscle's ability to produce optimal force. *Visualize a fighter trying to throw a punch into a heavy bag, but they are too close or too far away to land it with optimal force.

Reciprocal Inhibition: The simultaneous contraction of one muscle and the relaxation of its antagonist which allows movement to take place. The muscles on one side of a joint relax to allow the muscle on the other side to contract appropriately. *Agonist contract / Antagonist relax *Biceps contract, triceps relax, and vice versa.

Altered reciprocal inhibition *(altered length-tension)*: Process by which a short muscle, a tight muscle, and/or myofascial adhesions in the muscle cause decreased neural drive of its function antagonist. *Tight hip flexors decrease the neural drive to the gluteus maximus inhibiting their function. This causes synergistic dominance where the synergist (hamstrings) take over to perform the movement.

Force-Couple Relationship: Muscle groups moving together to produce movement around a joint. *The glutes, quads, and calf muscles work in a force couple to extend the hip and knee joints during walking or running. *Altered force-couple relationships cause synergistic dominance.

Synergistic Dominance *(altered force-couples)* Describes when synergists take over function for weak or inhibited prime movers. This is the result of improper recruitment patterns of muscle. *Understanding and identifying synergistic dominance will help you cue clients into better form.

Arthrokinematic dysfunction *(altered joint motion)*: Caused by altered length-tension relationships and force-couple relationships that affect the joints and leads to abnormal joint movement and proprioception causing poor movement efficiency.

Autogenic inhibition is the process by which neural impulses that sense tension (GTO) are greater than the impulses that cause muscles to contract (muscle spindles), providing an inhibitory effect to the muscle. * *Muscle spindles (contract)* ↔ *Golgi tendon organs (relax).* Activation of a Golgi tendon organ (GTO) inhibits a muscle spindle response, causing the muscle to relax after a stretch is held. An initial static stretch *(low-force)* causes a temporary increase in muscle tension *(low-grade)*. As the stretch is held a *stress-relaxation response* occurs gradually releasing tension after about 10 seconds.

Muscular Imbalance

Muscle Imbalance is the alteration of muscle length surrounding a joint. Think of it like a *Tug-of-War between opposing muscles (agonist / antagonist).* The overactive *(strong)* muscle wins and pulls the limb or body part into an altered *(unwanted)* position.

Muscle imbalances can be caused in a variety of ways:

- Postural stress
- Emotional duress
- Repetitive movement
- Cumulative trauma
- Poor training technique
- Lack of core strength
- Lack of neuromuscular efficiency

Overactive muscle: A state of having disrupted neuromuscular recruitment patterns that lead a muscle to be more active during a joint action.

* Overactive muscles are Shortened, Tight, and Strong (also called Hypertonic).

Underactive muscle: A state of having disrupted neuromuscular recruitment patterns that lead a muscle to be relatively less active during a joint action.

* Underactive muscles are Lengthened, Inhibited, and Weak (also called Hypotonic).

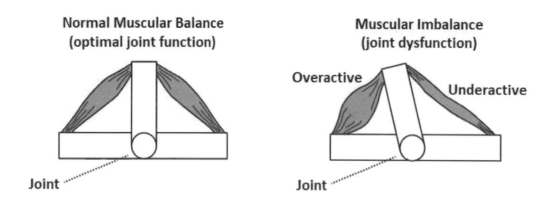

Once imbalances have been identified, overactive muscles should be lengthened, and underactive muscles strengthened to restore proper length-tension relationships.

There is a blog on our website that goes over *Overactive / Underactive Muscles. Everything you need to know* → www.cptprep.com/single-post/9-21-18

Muscle Action Definitions

Isometric (static) muscle action occurs when the contractile force of the muscle is *equal to the resistive force.* Isometric activation is when a muscle develops tension while maintaining a constant length. Dynamically stabilizes force, *Joints do not move.* *Think of a plank or a wall sit, the muscles are activated but there is no movement.* **Isometric** exercises strengthen muscle within **15 degrees** of the position held.

Concentric muscle action occurs when the contractile force of a muscle is *greater than the resistive force.* Shortening portion of muscle contraction where joint movement occurs. Concentric actions accelerate or produce force. Concentric activation moves *in the opposite direction of the force or resistance*. *Concentric means together, toward the center.*

*Learn a muscle's concentric muscle action to remember its isolated function. The biceps contract to flex the elbow joint. *Perform the movements to help memorize muscle function.*

Eccentric muscle action occurs when a muscle develops tension while lengthening. Eccentric activation occurs when the contractile force of a muscle is *less than the resistive force.* Eccentric activation slows movement, *"applying the brakes"* to decelerate force and maintain control. Eccentric actions move in the *same direction as the resistance*. *The lowering portion of a pull-up or squat.*

Incorporating exercises that challenge a muscle's *eccentric function* may help prevent injury during many functional movements. The hamstrings have to eccentrically decelerate when we come to a stop, or change in direction while running. If an athlete or individual can effectively *"apply the brakes"* when stopping or changing direction, then they reduce their chance of injury. A slow tempo during the eccentric portion of a Single-Leg Romanian deadlift is an excellent way to build up this ability to apply the brakes through eccentric strength control of the hamstrings.

Active Muscle Force: Muscle tension that is generated by its contractile elements through the neuromuscular system *(sliding filament theory).*

Passive Muscle Force: A muscle that is placed in a stretched position creates a passive force that can be utilized during contraction *(stretch-shortening cycle).*

Isotonic: Same tone throughout a movement.

Isokinetic: Same speed throughout a movement.

Isolated function: A muscle's primary function. A muscle action produced at a joint when a muscle is being concentrically activated to produce an acceleration of a body segment.

Integrated function: The coordination of muscles to produce, reduce, and stabilize forces in multiple planes for efficient and safe movement. *Inclusive of all muscle functions (concentric, isometric, eccentric).*

All or Nothing Principle

The All or Nothing Principle states that **motor units** cannot vary the amount of force they generate, they either contract maximally or not at all. A **single motor unit** consists of one **motor neuron (nerve)** and the **muscle fibers it innervates or activates.** For example, muscles involved with eye movement can have as little as 10 – 20 muscle fibers within each motor unit allowing for fine motor control of eye movements. Whereas large prime mover muscles of the legs and back can have thousands of muscle fibers connected to one motor unit.

Think of it like a power cord where you have a TV, cable box, and internet router all plugged into the same power source. Once you hit the switch, they all get power simultaneously.

A single muscle can have a million muscle fibers controlled by hundreds of motor units. This is why picking up a pencil can be done with minimal force but lifting a heavy dumbbell requires that additional motor units be recruited. The nervous system uses recruitment as a mechanism to efficiently utilize a skeletal muscle by activating only the motor units required to move the resistance applied. When necessary, the maximal number of motor units in a muscle can be recruited simultaneously, producing the maximum force of contraction for that muscle. A maximal strength contraction cannot last for very long because the energy requirements are very high to sustain.

Force-Velocity Curve

The Force-Velocity Curve states that as the velocity of a contraction increases, the concentric force decreases, and eccentric force increases. So we produce less force as the muscle shortens or contracts. Think of a push movement like a bench press or pull movement like a pull up on the last few reps when the pace slows. It may be difficult to reach the end range or get your chin over the bar, but once the rep is completed there is still a lot of eccentric capability to lower the weight or body slowly.

Neuromuscular efficiency is the ability of our neuromuscular system to produce and reduce force and stabilize the kinetic chain in all three planes of motion. ***Coordination***

Altered neuromuscular efficiency: Occurs when the kinetic chain is not performing optimally to control the body in all three planes of motion.

Structural efficiency refers to the structural alignment of the muscular and skeletal systems that allow our **center of gravity** to be maintained over our **base of support.** *Maintains balance*

Functional efficiency: The ability of the neuromuscular system to perform functional tasks with the least amount of energy, decreasing stress on the body's structure. *Functional efficiency is a result of structural efficiency.*

Intermuscular coordination: The ability of the neuromuscular system to allow all muscles to work together with proper activation and timing.

Muscle Movement Term Definitions

- **Agonist**: Muscles that work as the prime mover during movement / joint action. *Biceps are agonist during a bicep curl. *Agonist perform concentric activation.*

- **Antagonist**: Muscles that oppose the prime mover during movement / joint action. *Triceps are antagonist during a bicep curl. *Antagonist perform eccentric activation.*

- **Synergist**: Muscles that assist the prime mover during movement / joint action. *The hamstrings are synergist to the glutes during hip extension. *Synergist help the prime movers perform more efficiently.*

- **Stabilizer**: Muscles that minimize unwanted movement while the agonist and synergists work to provide movement at the joint. *The core muscles are stabilizers during all movement.*

Muscle Term Definitions

- **Hypertrophy**: Increase in the size of muscle fibers
- **Hyperplasia**: Increase in the number of muscle fibers
- **Atrophy**: Decrease in muscle fibers
- **DOMS**: Delayed Onset Muscle Soreness

Location and Function of Muscles

- **Origin**: The relatively stationary attachment site where the skeletal muscle begins.
- **Insertion**: The relatively mobile attachment site.
- **Muscle belly**: The mid-region in between the origin and insertion.
- **Line of pull**: The direction in which a muscle is pulled.
- **Parallel muscle**: Muscle with fibers that are oriented parallel to that muscle's longitudinal axis. *The rectus abdominis (abs) run parallel to their origin and insertion points.*
- **Pennate muscle**: Muscle with fibers that are oriented at an angle to the muscle's longitudinal axis. *Like a feather, it fans out from the origin and insertion. The calf muscle is an example.*

A **monoarticulate** muscle crosses one joint. A **biarticulate** muscle crosses two joints.

Tables 9-4 through 9-11 from Pages 341 – 346 of the Exercise Professional's Guide to Personal Training summarize the major skeletal muscles and their associated primary functions.

Muscle Locations by Area of the Body

Neck: Levator Scapulae, Sternocleidomastoid, Scalenes, Longus Coli, Longus Capitis

Shoulder / Chest (Anterior): Pectoralis Major and Minor, Anterior Deltoid, Medial Deltoid, Serratus Anterior

Shoulder / Back (Posterior): Upper, Middle, and Lower Trapezius, Rhomboid Major and Minor, Posterior Deltoid, Teres Major

Arms: Biceps Brachii, Triceps Brachii, Brachioradialis, Brachialis

Back: Superficial Erector Spinae *(Iliocostalis, Longissimus, Spinalis),* Quadratus Lumborum, Multifidus, Latissimus Dorsi

Core (Abdominal): Rectus abdominis, Internal and External Oblique, Transverse Abdominis, Diaphragm

Hip: Adductor Longus, Adductor Magnus *(anterior and posterior fibers),* Adductor Brevis, Gracilis, Pectineus, Gluteus Medius, Gluteus Minimus, Gluteus Maximus, Piriformis, Tensor Fascia Latae (TFL), Iliacus, Psoas, Sartorius

Hip flexor complex: Iliacus, Psoas, Sartorius, Rectus Femoris, Pectineus, Tensor Fascia Latae

Quadriceps: Vastus Lateralis, Vastus Intermedius, Vastus Medialis, Rectus Femoris

Hamstring complex: Biceps Femoris *(long a short heads),* Semimembranosus, Semitendinosus

Lower Leg (Anterior/front): Anterior Tibialis, Peroneus Longus

Lower Leg (Posterior/Calf): Posterior Tibialis, Soleus, Gastrocnemius

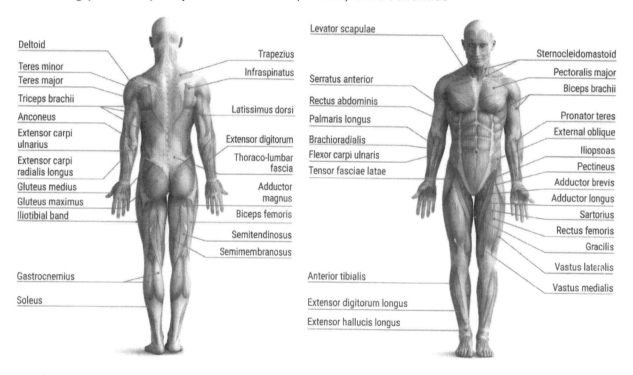

We have **5 FREE Anatomy websites** linked on our **Personal Trainer Resources blog** that show muscle locations and attachments, along with the skeletal and nervous systems.
www.cptprep.com/single-post/resources

Cardiorespiratory System

The **cardiorespiratory system** is composed of two separate systems that work together to provide energy for our bodies and carry away waste products.

> ➤ **Cardiovascular system *(circulatory)*:** Composed of the *heart, blood, and blood vessels.* The cardiovascular system provides the following (3) functions: ***Transportation, Regulation, and Protection.***

> ➤ **Respiratory system**: Composed of the *lungs, airways, and respiratory muscles such as the diaphragm.* The respiratory system collects oxygen from the external environment *(by inhaling air)* and transports it to the bloodstream through a process called ***diffusion.***

Cardiovascular System

The Heart is composed of four chambers, blood flows through the heart in the following order: ***Right Atrium, Right Ventricle, Left Atrium, and Left Ventricle.*** Think of the heart as two separate pumps with two champers in each. *The **atriums collect** the blood* and *the **ventricles pump** the blood.*

In addition to the heart chambers, four heart valves maintain blood flow in a single direction. Blood flows through the valves in the following order:

- **Tricuspid Valve**: Prevents backflow of blood into the right atrium.
- **Pulmonic Valve**: Prevents backflow of blood into the right ventricle.
- **Mitral (Bicuspid) Valve**: Prevents backflow of blood into the left atrium.
- **Aortic Valve**: Prevents backflow of blood into the left ventricle.

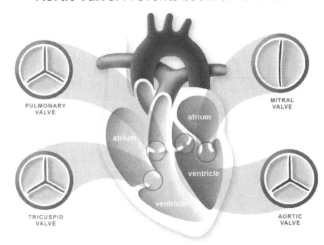

The Sinoatrial (SA) node is known as the ***pacemaker of the heart.*** This is where the electrical impulse that causes the heart to beat originates.

The Atrioventricular (AV) node is responsible for delaying the electrical impulses between the atria and the ventricles**. *This allows the atriums to fill with blood.*** After a brief pause of 0.12 sec, the electrical impulse moves through the heart bundle branches to contract the ventricles.

Blood Vessels are hollow tubes that allow blood to be transported from the heart, throughout the body, and back to the heart, creating a closed circuit. There are (3) major types of blood vessels:

- **Arteries (red)**: Carry blood **away** from the heart. As arteries get further away from the heart they become smaller and form small terminal branches called **arterioles**, which end in **capillaries.**

- **Capillaries** are the smallest blood vessels that form a network between the arteries and veins. This is where the exchange of water and gas between blood and tissues occurs.

- **Veins (blue)**: Carry blood **toward** the heart. Veins merge into smaller vessels called **venules** which collect blood from **capillaries**.

Figure 8-1a on page 252 and Figure 8-1b on page 253 of the Exercise Professional's Guide to Personal Training show a diagram of the major arteries and veins of the body.

Notice that the **arteries are shown in red** and the **veins are shown in blue.** This color-coding is helpful to remember which is which. **Red** blood cells are responsible for carrying oxygen to the body so the arteries are shown in red. **Veins** are responsible for carrying deoxygenated blood back to the lungs and heart. The color **blue is associated with a lack of oxygen,** such as blue lips or fingernails. Varicose veins typically seen in the lower leg of older individuals are also blue.

Blood is a life-sustaining fluid that circulates through our **heart** and **blood vessels**. It carries oxygen, nutrients, and hormones to all parts of our body. Blood also helps to regulate body temperature, fight infections, and remove waste products.

There are (3) types of cells in our blood: **Red Blood Cells / White Blood Cells / Platelets.**

Red blood cells carry oxygen from the lungs throughout the body, White blood cells help fight infection, and platelets help with clotting. These cells are suspended in a watery liquid called **Plasma.**

Heart Rate (HR) is measured by the number of beats or contractions of the heart in 1 minute *(Beats per minute)* **Resting heart rate (RHR)** is the number of BPM while the body is at rest. *True RHR is measured just before a person gets out of bed in the morning while still lying down.*

- A normal resting heart rate is between 60-100 BPM *(Beats per Minute)*.
- The average resting heart rate is between 60-80 BPM.
- **Bradycardia** is a term that indicates a heart rate that is slower than 60 BPM.
- **Tachycardia** is a heart rate that is faster than 100 BPM.

A person with a ***lower resting heart rate*** may indicate a ***higher fitness level***. An increase in stroke volume as a result of cardiovascular adaptations to exercise reduces the heart rate. ***Higher resting heart rates*** can be indicative of ***poor physical fitness.***

RHR is influenced by *fitness status, fatigue, body composition, body position, digestion, drugs, medication, alcohol, caffeine, and stress.* Clients should abstain from taking non-prescription stimulants or depressants for at least 12 hours prior to measuring their RHR.

Taking a 5 day average of RHR each morning and will provide a client's true RHR. Knowing a client's resting heart rate (RHR) provides insight into target heart rates for training and ***signs of overtraining*** when their ***RHR is elevated more than 5 BPM above baseline.***

- **Max Heart Rate (MHR)**: 220 – Age = MHR or 208 – (0.7 x Age) = MHR
  30-year-old would have Max HR of 190 BPM | 220 – 30 = 190 BPM

- **Heart Rate Reserve (HRR):** Max HR – Resting HR = HRR
  30 year old with resting HR of 60 BPM | 190 - 60 = 130 BPM

- **Target Heart Rate (THR)** = HRR x % Intensity + Resting HR **(Karvonen Formula)**
  30 year old mentioned above to train at 80% intensity | 130 x 0.80 + 60 = 164 BPM (THR)

Figure 7-1 and 7-2 on page 223 of the Exercise Professional's Guide to Personal Training show common heart rate sites. These include the radial artery and the carotid artery.

The ***recommended location*** to measure heart rate *(pulse)* is at the ***radial artery*** which is on the thumb side of the wrist just below the palm. A good way to remember this location is to give thumbs up and turn your hand like you are pointing your thumb at someone next to you *(to the right)*. Your thumb and forearm make the shape of a *lower case "r"*. This indicates the side of the arm where the ***radius bone*** and ***radial artery*** are located ***(both beginning with the letter r).*** You would count the number of heart beats in 6 seconds and add a zero to that number.

If you keep your hand in this position with your thumb out and put your pinky up in a ***Hang Loose sign*** *(like surfers do)* it sort of makes ***the shape of a "U".*** The Ulna bone *(other bone in the forearm)* is located on the pinky side of the wrist. This is a good way to remember the bones in the lower arm and the preferred location for a manual heart rate measurement.

Stroke Volume (SV) is the amount of blood ejected from the left ventricle of the heart in a single contraction. SV is lower in an upright posture *(standing up)* in untrained individuals compared to trained individuals. SV also increases in the supine or prone positions *(lying down)*.

Cardiac Output (Q) measures the overall performance of the heart. It measures the amount of blood pumped by the heart per minute in liters using the following formula:

> ➢ **Heart Rate (HR) x Stroke Volume (SV) = Cardiac Output (Q)**

At rest, cardiac output averages approximately *5 liters per minute.* During maximal exercise, this number increases to *20 – 25 liters per minute* and up to *30 – 40 liters* in highly trained individuals. *Cardiac output (Q) increases linearly with exercise intensity.*

Blood Pressure (BP) is the result of the amount of blood pumped from the heart *(cardiac output)* and the resistance the flow of blood meets at the vessels. **Blood pressure is defined as the pressure of the circulating blood against the walls of the blood vessels *(measured in millimeters of mercury.)***

> ➢ **Systolic blood pressure (SBP)** is the pressure exerted on the arteries during the contraction phase of the heart *(when the heart beats).* *SBP increases linearly with exercise intensity. A SBP that fails to rise or falls with increasing workloads may signal a plateau or decrease in cardiac output (Q).*

> ➢ **Diastolic blood pressure (DBP)** is the pressure exerted on the arteries during the relaxation phase of the heart *(in between beats)* *Diastolic BP is **determined** when the pulse **fades away**. *DBP may decrease slightly or remain unchanged with exercise intensity.*

Blood Pressure Categories

BLOOD PRESSURE CATEGORY	SYSTOLIC mm Hg (upper number)		DIASTOLIC mm Hg (lower number)
NORMAL	LESS THAN 120	and	LESS THAN 80
ELEVATED	120 – 129	and	LESS THAN 80
HIGH BLOOD PRESSURE (HYPERTENSION) STAGE 1	130 – 139	or	80 – 89
HIGH BLOOD PRESSURE (HYPERTENSION) STAGE 2	140 OR HIGHER	or	90 OR HIGHER
HYPERTENSIVE CRISIS (consult your doctor immediately)	HIGHER THAN 180	and/or	HIGHER THAN 120

Respiratory System

The **respiratory system (pulmonary)** is composed of the *nose, nasal cavity, airways (pharynx, larynx, trachea, bronchi) lungs, and respiratory muscles* that help us breathe. This system is responsible for collecting oxygen from the external environment *(by inhaling air)* and removing carbon dioxide from the body *(by exhaling air).* It also makes speech possible and plays an important role in regulating acid-base balance during exercise.

Figure 8-3 on page 255 of the Exercise Professional's Guide to Personal Training shows a diagram of the upper and lower respiratory pathways.

Inspiration *(Inhalation)* occurs by contracting our inspiratory muscles to move air into the lungs.

- **Primary muscles *(at rest)*** include the diaphragm, and external intercostals *(muscles between the ribs)*

- **Secondary muscles *(during exercise)*** include the pectoralis minor, scalenes, sternocleidomastoid *(these are muscles of the neck and chest)*

Expiration *(exhalation)* can either be ***passive*** by relaxing our inspiratory muscles or ***active*** by contracting our expiratory muscles to move air out.

- **Expiratory muscles** include the internal intercostals, abdominals, internal obliques, and serratus posterior. *(muscles of the core)*

Figure 8-4 on page 256 of the Exercise Professional's Guide to Personal Training shows a diagram of the diaphragm and intercostal muscles.

Think about breathing patterns during exercise, especially during resistance training when lifting a heavier weight. We ***inhale*** during the ***eccentric*** portion of the lift. This would be the lowering portion of a bench press, squat, or pull-up. Then we typically do a ***controlled exhale*** during the ***concentric*** portion of the lift as we contract our muscles to move the resistance. *(Pursed lip like blowing through a straw, or exhaling slowly through the teeth).*

The reason for this is that an ***active exhale activates the muscles of our core.*** This provides stability to allow our bodies to perform the movement more safely and effectively. ***"Proximal Stability promotes Distal Mobility."*** If our core is stable, then we can move our limbs more efficiently. This is a good mental anchor to keep in mind.

Cardiorespiratory Fitness is defined as the capacity of the heart and lungs to deliver blood and oxygen to the working muscles during exercise. ***Oxygen uptake or consumption*** depends on the ***respiratory system's*** ability to take in oxygen and the ***cardiovascular system's*** ability to transport it to the tissues of the body.

- **Resting oxygen consumption (VO^2)** 3.5 ml × kg-1 × min-1 = 1 metabolic equivalent(MET)
- **Maximal oxygen consumption (VO^2Max)** is the highest rate of oxygen transport and utilization achieved at maximal physical exertion.

VO^2Max is the best measure of cardiorespiratory fitness. However, it's hard to directly measure without expensive equipment. Submaximal exercise test to predict VO2 Max can be used. These include the *Rockport Walk Test, the Step Test, and the YMCA bike protocol.*

> ➤ **VO^2Max** usually peaks and plateaus after about **6 months of regular training.**

With regular exercise, our **ventilatory threshold *(lactate threshold)*** may continue to **increase for years.** This occurs primarily due to ***capillary growth and increased mitochondrial density in the active muscles***. The muscle's ability to store additional glycogen for energy and use fatty acids as a fuel source is also enhanced.

Abnormal or dysfunctional breathing decreases our functional capacity and is associated with ***stress and anxiety***. Shallow chest breathing using mostly the secondary muscles causes tension and can alter the blood oxygen and carbon dioxide content. This may result in headaches, fatigue, poor circulation, and/or poor sleep patterns. If a client complains of any of these symptoms you should ***refer them to a medical professional.***

This is a good time to mention that it's important to watch a client's breathing pattern as they exercise. People who are new to exercise tend to tense up and hold their breath as they approach the end of a set. It's always important to cue them to breathe and talk them through the exercise while making sure they maintain proper form. ***Inhaling during the eccentric portion and controlled exhales on the concentric.***

Below is a Recap of the entire process of the ***cardiorespiratory system.*** Think about these systems as you read along and begin to consciously breathe.

We ***inhale*** air into our lungs. Our lungs ***diffuse*** the oxygen 0^2 into our bloodstream. The ***left*** atrium of our heart receives this oxygenated blood from our lungs, and the ***left ventricle pumps*** this oxygenated blood to all parts of our body through our ***arteries***. Once our bodies use this oxygen, our cells produce carbon dioxide. The ***right atrium*** collects this deoxygenated blood from the body through our ***veins***, the ***right ventricle*** then ***pumps*** this blood to the lungs. Our lungs ***diffuse*** the carbon dioxide $C0^2$ made by our cells and remove it from our body as we ***exhale*** it back into the environment. This entire process happens in one single breath!

Domain II: Program Design and Implementation

Create individualized programs that promote healthy behaviors through exercise, nutrition, education, and coaching.

The following provides a summary of the **ACE Integrated Fitness Training Model (ACE IFT)** which is a registered trademark of the *American Council on Exercise.* For additional information see **Chapter 2 from pages 35 – 53 of the Exercise Professional's Guide to Personal Training.** The ACE IFT Model has two principal training components that are divided into three phases.

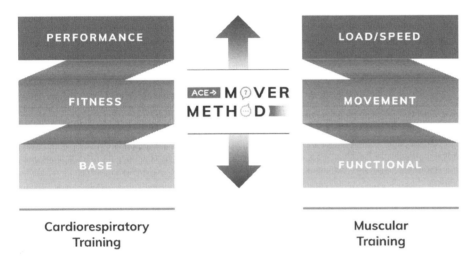

The **Function-Health-Fitness-Performance Continuum** states that exercise programs should follow a progression to first reestablish proper function, then improve health, then develop and advance fitness, and finally enhance performance. Human movement and fitness can **progress and regress** along this spectrum. Each of your clients will be at a unique point on this continuum based on their current health status, lifestyle factors, and activity level. This is why it's so important to **meet your clients where they currently are (both mentally and physically)** so that you can help them progress based on their **goals, needs, and abilities.**

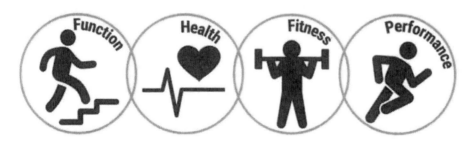

The ACE IFT Model allows trainers to develop individualized programs for clients ranging from sedentary to athletes. Clients are categorized into a given phase based on their current health, fitness level, and goals. **Rapport** *is the foundation for success in all phases of the ACE IFT Model.*

ACE Mover Method and ABC Approach

> **Asking open-ended questions** Step 1 is to ask powerful starter questions to identify what the client hopes to accomplish by working with an exercise professional.

> **Breaking down barriers** Step 2 is to ask probing questions to discover what potential obstacles may get in the way of the client reaching his or her specific goals.

> **Collaborating** Step 3 is to collaborate to set *SMART goals* and establish specific action steps toward those goals.

Throughout the ACE Guide in each chapter, they give great real-world scenarios using the *ACE Mover Method* and the *ABC Approach*. We highly recommend reading through these as you study and not skip over them as they provide some solid practical advice for dealing with various clients and situations.

The ACE Integrated Fitness Training Model provides personal trainers with a systematic approach to training. Programming in each phase will be based on the **three-zone intensity model** using various intensity markers. *Table 8-11 from pages 305 – 307 of the Exercise Professional's Guide to Personal Training* shows the three training zones and all of the methods of estimating exercise intensity for each zone *(Talk Test, RPE, VT1 and VT2, %MHR, %HRR, MET)* We highly recommend flagging these pages for future reference.

Clients may be in different phases of cardiorespiratory and muscular training based on their current health, fitness, exercise-participation levels, and goals. For example, an endurance athlete could be in the performance phase for cardiorespiratory training and the movement phase of muscular training. Whereas a powerlifter could be in the load / speed phase of muscular training and the base phase of cardiorespiratory training.

Six Steps for Client-centered Exercise Programing

> **Step 1**: Establish rapport and identify client goals

> **Step 2**: Administer an exercise preparticipation health screening

> **Step 3**: Identify barriers and collaborate on next steps *(ABC Approach)*

> **Step 4**: Determine if physiological or movement assessments are necessary

> **Step 5**: Determine in which phase(s) of the ACE IFT Model to begin

> **Step 6**: Prioritize program design and select exercise order

Ventilatory Threshold

Ventilatory threshold describes the point of transition between predominately aerobic energy production to anaerobic energy production.

The **First ventilatory threshold (VT1)** is the *"crossover"* point which represents a level of intensity at which blood lactate accumulates faster than it can be cleared. This causes us to breathe faster in an effort to blow off the extra CO_2 that is produced. The *"talk test" (if a person can talk comfortably in sentences while performing the exercise)* is a good indicator that someone is training below VT1.

The **Second ventilatory threshold (VT2)** occurs at the point of intensity where blowing off the CO_2 is no longer adequate to buffer the rapidly increasing lactate. High-intensity exercise *(≥VT2)* can only be sustained for a brief period due to the accumulation of lactate.

A person's heart rate can be determined at both their VT1 and VT2 thresholds by using the Submaximal talk test for VT1 and VT2 threshold testing.

> ➤ **Submaximal Talk Test for VT1** protocol listed from *pages 299 – 301 of the Exercise Professional's Guide to Personal Training*. A treadmill, elliptical, cycle ergometer or arm ergometer can be used since they are easy to track HR and maintain a steady pace.

> ➤ **VT2 Threshold Testing** is only recommended for well-conditioned individuals with fitness and performance goals. Protocol listed from *pages 301– 302 of the Exercise Professional's Guide to Personal Training. 15 – 20 min of steady high-intensity is performed and then 95% of that average HR during activity is used to estimate the VT2 threshold.*

VT1 and VT2 metabolic markers can be used to divide training intensity into the following three zones.

> ➤ **Zone 1** (low to moderate exercise) reflects intensity below VT1

> ➤ **Zone 2** (moderate to vigorous exercise) reflects intensity above VT1 to just below VT2

> ➤ **Zone 3** (vigorous to very vigorous exercise) reflects intensity at or above VT2

Cardiorespiratory Training

Pages 42 – 45 in Chapter 2 and pages 470 – 476 in Chapter 11 of the Exercise Professional's Guide to Personal Training covers the cardiorespiratory training phases of the ACE IFT Model.

Phase 1: Base Training (Below VT1)

ACE Fitness mission statement is to **"get people moving."** The beginning stages of a program should be focused on building positive experiences for the client and **"small wins"** along the way to motivate them for life long exercise adherence. Think of the common phrases **"Aim to be 1% better every day"** or **"Better than the person you were yesterday."** (whether it's more resilient, stronger, smarter, or healthier in any way)

Focusing on these small **"task-oriented"** incremental changes consistently will build the **compound gains** in mental and physical capacity down the line, as the tangible changes start to surface. Initial cardiorespiratory fitness assessments are not necessary in the base training level. Remember, we want our clients to have **positive associations with exercise.** Putting a deconditioned client through a cardiorespiratory assessment early on in a training program could potentially **serve as a negative reminder of their current level of fitness** and reduce their self-efficacy.

This training phase establishes the foundation for aerobic fitness and health that is built upon in the following stages. Exercise during this phase should be performed at steady-state intensities in the low-to-moderate range. The goal of this phase is to gradually increase duration and frequency until the client can complete **20 – 30 minutes of moderate-intensity for 3 – 5 days per week.** Zone 1 Base Training is below the **"Talk Test" threshold**, which is the crossover point for the **first ventilatory threshold (VT1).** Once they have achieved an acceptable aerobic base they are ready to progress to the fitness training stage and cardio assessments if warranted. ***Do not increase more than 10% duration from the prior week.**

Typically, a phase of **training lasts about 4 weeks** as this is the timeframe for most adaptations to occur. However, **base training** could be **as little as 2 weeks or up to 6 weeks in duration** depending on your client's current fitness level.

*A study showed that training at intensities less than 50% of HRR failed to cause reductions in RHR and increases in VO2Max However, the Base Level of training is still sufficient for health improvements and reduction in the controllable chronic diseases mentioned in Chapter 1 and it is an important starting point for deconditioned individuals.

Phase 2: Fitness Training (Above VT1 Below VT2)

Fitness training includes modifying the variables of the FITT-VP principle *(frequency, volume (duration), and intensity) while* incorporating *intervals* that go into zone 2 and eventually approach the second ventilatory threshold VT2. This is an appropriate time to perform the submaximal talk test to determine your client's heart rate at the VT1 threshold. As a person increases their cardiorespiratory capacity and efficiency, they can train at higher intensities with a lower heart rate. Therefore, the submaximal talk test should be reassessed periodically to adjust their heart rate value at the VT1 threshold. The goal of aerobic intervals is to improve aerobic endurance and increase the client's ability to use fat as a fuel source.

Phase 3: Performance Training (Above VT2)

Zone 3 performance training is designed for clients who have endurance-performance or competitive goals such as achieving a personal best or competing against other individuals in endurance-related activities. This is an appropriate time to perform the VT2 threshold assessment.

Incorporating HIIT training can help increase anaerobic power. A short burst of high intensity followed by rest periods. This type of high-intensity training is usually performed *1 – 2 times per week to allow for adequate recovery.*

Even elite level athletes only perform a small amount of their training in Zone 3 (roughly 5 – 10% of total training). This is *based on the inverse relationship between intensity and duration.* If the intensity is high the duration will be short and as the intensity decreases the duration can last much longer. Proper recovery and rest must also be implemented in Zone 3 training to allow adaptations to occur and prevent overtraining or injury.

It seems that the best benefit to overall fitness is to *train in Zone 1 80% of total training time, and Zone 3 10% of the time, with overlapping Zone 2 bouts that cross both thresholds.* Mostly training just at or below VT1 with short bouts just above VT2 seem to garner the highest cardio benefit.

Muscular Training

Pages 46 – 50 in Chapter 2 and pages 477 – 510 in Chapter 11 of the Exercise Professional's Guide to Personal Training covers the muscular training phases of the ACE IFT Model.

Phase 1: Functional Training

This phase sets the foundation for the phases that follow. Focus on restoring and/or maintaining the client's normal joint alignment, joint movement, muscle balance, and muscle function. Assessments of the client's posture, balance, movement, range of motion of the ankle, hip, shoulder complex, thoracic, and lumbar spine should be performed in the early stages of this phase of training. You can then implement an exercise program that addresses the client's weaknesses and imbalances found during these assessments. The goal of this phase is to develop the client's postural stability and proper movement patterns. Exercise programs should improve *muscular endurance, flexibility, core function, and static and dynamic balance*.

"Straighten the body before you Strengthen it" This concept is emphasized in the assessment stage and early part of a training program. We must observe our client's posture and movement patterns to ensure that proper technique is being used at each training session. *If resistance is added to faulty movement patterns it can cause further muscular imbalances and may lead to injury.* If imbalances are present then corrective exercises are often incorporated into the warm-up and cool-down portions and on off training days.

If a muscle is overactive it's going to inhibit the antagonist *(muscle on the opposing side)*. *Think of it like a light switch with a dimmer on it.* When working optimally, the muscle is signaled by the nervous system and full activation occurs, but when a muscle is inhibited by its antagonist or lengthened and weak it does not get the full signal from the nervous system. It's like turning a light on its lowest dim setting. *The signal is reduced therefore the contraction is reduced.*

"Proximal Stability promotes Distal Mobility" Proximal means towards the center describing our core, which is made up of the structures of the **Lumbo-Pelvic-Hip-Complex (LPHC)**. This includes *the lumbar spine, the pelvic girdle, abdomen, and the hip joint*. The core is where our *center of gravity (COG)* is and where all movement originates. A stable core allows for efficient movement of our *distal segments (arms and legs)*. Imagine trying to swing a baseball bat, or throw a punch or kick without stabilizing your core. When our core is braced and stabilized it *creates a fulcrum point* which helps to *create torque and enhance movement*. Stabilize the core and lumbar area, and then progress to mobility of the more distal segments.

> ➤ **Stability** is the ability to prepare, maintain, anticipate, and restore stability at each joint.

> ➤ **Mobility** is the range of uninhibited movement around a joint or body segment.

Building up a stable core can be done using the *drawing-in maneuver, abdominal bracing, and working the hollow position. Planks, side planks, glute bridges, supermans, dead-bugs, and bird dogs are also great options for building proximal stability.*

Keeping these concepts in mind is a good way to walk through the function of the human body and logical training progression. ***Straighten and Stabilize the body and then work to build strength and power off of that solid foundation.*** Restoring proper joint alignment and muscle balance along with ***proper execution of the five primary movement patterns*** sets the foundation for the subsequent phases of training.

It's important even for well-trained individuals to incorporate a ***"Body Maintenance Routine."*** Periodically checking in on our base strength and function helps keep the body optimal. Working in a daily stability and movement routine in the morning or at night before bed can be very beneficial. ***10 – 15 minutes of maintenance a day will help keep the injuries away.***

Table 15-4 on Page 709 of the Exercise Professional's Guide to Personal Training shows a chart of select muscle groups and their contributions to trunk and pelvic stability.

Balance Training is another component of Functional Training as it challenges the stabilizing muscles to promote kinetic chain stability and joint mobility. ***Balance training is recommended to be performed 3 days per week for 10 – 15 minutes each session.***

Figure 11-15 on Page 488 of the Exercise Professional's Guide to Personal Training gives example balance progressions. Appropriate balance training progressions are as follows:

- Two-leg stable
- Single-leg stable
- Two-leg unstable
- Single-leg unstable

Balance training is performed in ***proprioceptively enriched environments*** that are unstable, yet controllable. These are used to teach the body how to recruit the right muscle, at the right time, with the right amount of force.

This type of balance training ***improves force production*** and ***injury prevention.***

Phase 2: Movement Training

Motor learning plays a big role in movement training, repetitions should be emphasized over exercise intensity. Drilling and practicing the movements downloads the pattern into our brain and nervous system. The timeframe for movement training depends on each client's initial level of movement ability and their rate of progression. It could last two weeks for one client and two months for another. **Movement Training** incorporates exercises that are categorized based on the following.

Five Primary Movement Patterns

1. *Bend-and-Lift movements*
2. *Single-Leg movements*
3. *Pushing movements*
4. *Pulling movements*
5. *Rotational movements*

When teaching clients bend-and-lift or single-leg movements, you should begin with **"arms down"** positions as **"high-arm"** positions require a greater degree of thoracic mobility which many clients may lack.

The need for thoracic mobility is greater during rotational movements given the three-dimensional nature of the movement patterns. Performing these movements without proper thoracic mobility or lumbar stability may compromise the shoulders and hips increasing the likelihood of injury.

Before adding resistance to movement patterns, the client must first demonstrate proficiency with the following:

Performing body-weight movement sequences with proper form, core stabilization, control of their center of gravity (COG), and control of the velocity of movement.

Movement is essential to complete all **Activities of daily living (ADL)** which are basic daily tasks such as self-care, and household chores. One's ability to perform these tasks has been correlated with balance, postural control, and joint mobility. Flexibility exercises along with resistance training can help to improve range of motion (ROM) within the joints as well as increase balance and postural stability.

Phase 3: Load / Speed Training

This phase applies external loads to the five primary movement patterns to increase _**muscular endurance, strength, and/or power**_ depending on the client's goals.

- ➢ **Endurance** is the ability of a muscle or muscle group to continually perform without fatigue _(measured by repeated or sustained muscle contractions)_.

- ➢ **Hypertrophy** is the increase in the size of muscle fibers.

- ➢ **Strength** is the ability of a muscle or muscle group to exert force _(usually measured by one-repetition maximum 1-RM)_.

- ➢ **Power** is the ability to exert force with speed. _Power = Force x Velocity_

**Body composition, movement function, health, and performance** also improve with resistance training. Functional movement exercises should be continued during the warm-up and cool-down phases to ensure the client maintains a solid base to build upon.

Performance training programs are designed to improve the motor skill-related components of physical fitness including _**speed, agility, quickness, reactivity, and power.**_ Clients who are interested in performance or power type training should be capable of _**acceleration (concentric), deceleration (eccentric) "applying the brakes", and stabilization (isometric)**_ during the powerful movements required for performance training. The pre-requisites include:

- ➢ A foundation of strength and joint integrity _(mobility and stability)_

- ➢ Adequate static balance and dynamic balance

- ➢ Effective core function

- ➢ Anaerobic efficiency _(training the anaerobic energy pathways)_

- ➢ Athleticism _(sufficient skills to perform advanced movements)_

- ➢ No contraindications for load-bearing, dynamic movements

- ➢ No medical concerns that affect balance and motor skills

Resistance exercises involving _**each major muscle group trained 2 – 3 days per week**_ is recommended. Multi-joint and Single-joint exercises can be used with a variety of exercise equipment and/or bodyweight. A rest of ≥48 hours between sessions for any single muscle group is recommended. A gradual progression of greater resistance, more repetitions per set, and/or increasing frequency is recommended.

Training Volume Based on Goals

Training volume is a good indication of energy used in a workout as there is a correlation between the total amount of weight lifted and the total number of calories burned.

➢ *Rep Volume = Reps x Sets*

➢ *Weight Lifted = Weight x Reps x Sets*

Training volume should be low in the beginning and gradually increase as the client develops adherence to the program. A person's current fitness status provides a good indicator of the appropriate volume. Deconditioned or novice clients should begin with manageable volumes before progressing to the training volumes outlined below. Advanced individuals may require additional *Frequency, Intensity, Time, and Volume* in order to obtain progressive results.

General Muscle Fitness

- *Sets*: 1 – 4 per exercise
- *Reps*: 8 – 15 per set
- *Rest*: 2 – 3 minutes seconds between sets
- *Intensity*: 20 – 70% of 1RM

Endurance

- *Sets*: 2 – 3 per exercise
- *Reps*: ≥ 12 per set
- *Rest*: ≤ 30 seconds between sets
- *Intensity*: ≤ 67% of 1RM

Hypertrophy

- *Sets*: 3 – 6 per exercise
- *Reps*: 6 – 12 per set
- *Rest*: 30 – 90 seconds between sets
- *Intensity*: 67 – 85% of 1RM

Strength

- *Sets*: 2 – 6 per exercise
- *Reps*: ≤ 6 per set
- *Rest*: 2 – 5 minutes between sets
- *Intensity*: ≥ 85% of 1RM

Power

- *Sets*: 3 – 5 per exercise
- *Reps*: 1 – 2 per set for single-effort events / 3 – 5 per set for multiple-effort events
- *Rest*: 2 – 5 minutes between sets
- *Intensity*: 80 – 90% of 1RM for single-effort / 75 – 85% of 1RM for multiple-effort

Common Resistance-Training Myths and Mistakes

- Fat deposits in certain areas *(the abdomen or thighs)* can be targeted with strength training via spot reduction. Remember the phrase *"First on, Last off"* fat deposits typically come off in the reverse order that they were stored.
- Women will build bulky muscles through weight training.
- Individuals should use light weights and high repetitions to improve muscle tone, and heavy weights and low repetitions to increase muscle mass.
- At some point, people get too old to lift weights.
- Children are too young to lift weights.
- Free weights are always better than machines.
- After a person stops resistance training, the muscle turns to fat.
- Strength training is bad for the exerciser's blood pressure.

Training Principles

Specificity of Training: Only the muscles that are trained will adapt and change in response.

> **SAID Principle**: Specific Adaptations to Imposed Demands

FITT-VP *(Frequency, Intensity, Time, Type, Volume, Pattern / Progression)* can be used to achieve the client's desired exercise goals *(favorable changes in body composition, muscular strength, muscular endurance, muscle hypertrophy, looking more "toned," etc.)*

Initially adjusting **exercise duration is the most appropriate variable**, and then once exercise adherence has been developed trainers can implement progression by increasing exercise **frequency and intensity.** *The FITT-VP principles should be applied to design Cardiorespiratory, Muscular, and Flexibility exercise programs*.

Progressive Overload states that as the body adapts to a given stimulus, an increase in stimulus is required for further adaptations and improvements.

Increasing repetitions and adding **resistance in 5% increments** *(whenever the end range number of reps can be completed)* are two principal approaches to strength-training progression. To maximize strength development, the resistance should be heavy enough to fatigue the target muscles within the limits of the **anaerobic energy system (90 seconds or less).** A general rep range of 8 – 12 is recommended as it falls within this timeframe. This rep range correlates to approximately 70 – 80% of a person's 1RM.

Even though clients may have specific goals for training it is important to also train all of the major muscle groups to reduce the risk of muscle imbalance and overuse injuries.

There are six motor skill-related components of physical fitness: Agility, Balance, Coordination, Reaction time, Speed, and Power.

Exercise Selection and Order

The *order of exercises* should be prioritized according to the *client's needs and goals*. A few ways to determine exercise selection is by grouping exercises based on *body area (hips, core), function (push / pull), or by relevance to activity or sport.*

Multi-joint exercise: Involves two or more muscle groups and joints during the exercise. *(Deadlifts, squats, and bench press are examples of multi-joint exercises)*

Single-joint exercise: Isolated muscle group exercises involving one joint movement. *(Bicep curls, knee extensions, and leg curls are some examples of single-joint exercises)*

Push exercises: Exercises involving the *"push"* muscle groups. *(Bench press, squats, abduction)*

Pull exercises: Exercises involving the *"pull"* muscle groups. *(Pull-ups, deadlifts, adduction)*

Unilateral: Exercises or movements involving one limb. *(One arm bicep curl is an example)*

Bilateral: Exercises or movements involving both limbs. *(Barbell bench press is an example)*

Greater strength gains are seen in the exercises that are performed first due to the greater number of reps and sets *(volume)* one can perform when they are fresh. Ideally, an exercise session should start with the largest muscle group or most complex exercise and progress to smaller muscle groups and less complex movements. The following are general recommendations when deciding the order of exercises:

➢ Large muscle groups before small muscle groups

➢ Multi-joint before single-joint exercises

➢ Alternate push/pull exercises for total body sessions

➢ Alternate upper/lower body exercises for total body sessions

➢ Explosive/power lifts and plyometric exercises before basic strength and single-joint

➢ Exercises for priority weak areas before exercises for strong areas

➢ Most intense to least intense

Tempos are usually 6 seconds per rep. *1 – 3 for concentric and 2 – 4 for eccentric.* Longer eccentric phases seem to correlate with increased potential for DOMS.

Rest Interval is the time taken between sets or exercises to rest or recover. Generally, rest intervals of 1 minute are sufficient.

Amount of Rest	Percent Recovery
30 seconds	50%
60 seconds	75%
2 minutes	95%
3 – 5 minutes	100%

Progression of Exercises

Describes the progressive stages of making an exercise more difficult or challenging. Usually by creating additional instability which enhances proprioception and neuromuscular control.

- Easy to Hard
- Slow to Fast
- Static to Dynamic
- Stable to Unstable
- Simple to Complex
- Eyes Open to Eyes Closed *(vestibular system)*
- Two Arms/Legs to Single-Arm/Leg
- Known to Unknown *(reactive capabilities)*
- Body Weight to Loaded Movements

Progressing an individual too quickly can lead to improper movement patterns and increase the risk of injury. A client must be able to perform an exercise with proper form and technique before progressing to a more challenging version or exercise

Regression of Exercises

Describes regressing an exercise making it easier to perform. Usually by creating a more stable base of support or decreasing the lever length.

If a client is unable to perform a standard push-up you could regress the movement to have them perform it with their knees on the ground instead. Once enough strength has been built-up they could progress to a traditional push-up and even further to performing push-ups with feet on a bench or stability ball.

Movements of major muscle groups (Biomechanics)

Biomechanics is the study of motion and causes of motion of living things. Biomechanical principles should be used during common physical activities such as walking, running, lifting, and carrying objects as well as resistance training.

Squats are a full-body multi-joint compound exercise. The gluteus maximus and quadriceps are the agonists *(prime movers),* and the hamstrings, erector spinae, transverse abdominis, gluteus medius/minimus, abductors, adductors, soleus, and gastrocnemius are the synergists and stabilizer *(secondary)* muscles involved during the squat.

The ***deadlift*** is another compound movement that works a variety of muscle groups. The erector spinae *(lower back)* are the agonist along with the gluteus maximus and hamstrings to extend the hip joint. The quadriceps also work to extend the knee joint. The adductor magnus works to stabilize the legs. The forearms and grip muscles of the hands hold the bar. The core muscles activate to help the erector spinae stabilize the spine during the movement.

The ***bench press*** is an upper-body compound movement. The agonist muscles of the bench press are pectoralis major and minor, anterior deltoids, and triceps. The antagonist muscles of the bench press are the biceps, posterior deltoids, rhomboids, and trapezius.

Spotting Techniques

Proper spotting techniques reassure the client while performing an exercise and reduce the risk of injury. It's good practice for trainers to provide a verbal explanation of the exercise along with a demonstration of proper lifting technique prior to the client performing the exercise. This will help the client visualize the movement and maintain proper position, form, technique, and control while performing the exercise. The following is a checklist for proper spotting technique:

- ➤ Know how many repetitions the client is going to do before performing the set.
- ➤ Make sure to have a good base of support and that you are strong enough to assist with the resistance being used.
- ➤ Stop your clients if they break form or have improper technique.
- ➤ Keep hands on or close to the weight being lifted but never take the weight away from the client unless they are in immediate danger of dropping or losing control.
- ➤ The aim is to provide just enough assistance for the client to successfully complete the lift, helping them through any *"sticking point."*
- ➤ **Spot at the client's forearms near the wrists when using dumbbells**, especially for chest press and overhead press exercises. Spotting at their elbows doesn't prevent the elbows from flexing and caving inward. **Certain exercises require spotting with hands on the dumbbell itself such as a dumbbell pullover or overhead dumbbell triceps extension.*

Methods of Estimating Exercise Intensity

VO$_2$ Max: Maximal oxygen consumption
With training VO$_2$ Max increases but reaches a peak and plateaus within about six months.
VO$_2$ Rest: Resting oxygen consumption (VO$_2$ Rest = 3.5)
VO$_2$ Reserve: Oxygen uptake reserve (VO$_2$ Reserve = VO$_2$ Max - 3.5)
Target VO$_2$ = VO$_2$ Max - VO$_2$ Rest x % of Intensity + VO$_2$Rest

Training programs based on the percent of VO$_2$ Max or VO$_2$ Reserve depend on an accurate maximal or submaximal exercise test to determine a person's true VO$_2$ Max. Given that maximal tests are rarely available, and equations for estimating VO$_2$ Max are not 100% accurate this technique is not recommended unless a person's VO$_2$ Max is directly measured.

MET: Metabolic Energy Equivalent is an index of energy expenditure. One MET is the rate of energy expenditure while at rest that is equal to an oxygen uptake *(VO$_2$) of 3.5.* ***Common physical activity MET values can be found in Table 8-8 on page 284 of the Exercise Professional's Guide to Personal Training.***

- VO$_2$ ÷ 3.5 = MET
- MET x 3.5 x Body Weight in Kg ÷ 200 = kcal *(Calories expended per minute formula)*

Max Heart Rate (MHR): 220 – Age = MHR or 208 – (0.7 x Age) = MHR
* *30-year-old would have Max HR of 190 BPM | 220 – 30 = 190 BPM*

Heart Rate Reserve (HRR): Max HR – Resting HR = HRR
* *30-year-old with resting HR of 60 BPM | 190 - 60 = 130 BPM*

Target Heart Rate (THR) = HRR x % Intensity + Resting HR **(Karvonen Formula)**
* *30-year-old mentioned above to train at 80% intensity | 130 x 0.80 + 60 = 164 BPM (THR)*

Ratings of Perceived Exertion (RPE)	
Classic Scale (6 – 20)	*Modern Scale (0 – 10)*
6	0 Nothing at all
7 Very, very light	0.5 Very, very weak
8	1 Very weak
9 Very light	2 Weak
10	3 Moderate
11 Fairly light	4 Somewhat strong
12	
13 Somewhat hard	5 Strong
14	6
15 Hard	7 Very strong
16	
17 Very hard	8
18	9
19 Very, very hard	10 Very, very strong
20	* Maximal

Energy Systems

Adenosine triphosphate (ATP) is a high-energy molecule that stores energy to be used in cellular and mechanical work. Our bodies break down ATP to release the energy for muscular contractions that move our body. Only about *40% of the energy released from ATP* is used, the *remaining 60% of that energy is released as heat.* This is why our body temperature increases during bouts of exercise.

Muscle fibers produce ATP by three pathways: Creatine phosphate (CP), Anaerobic Glycolysis, and Aerobic Oxidation. Think of these pathways as 3 separate systems that produce energy.

Anaerobic energy systems do not require oxygen to produce energy. They are the immediate short-term systems used in the first few minutes of exercise. ATP stored in muscle, Creatine Phosphate (PCr), and Anaerobic Glycolysis make up the anaerobic energy systems.

The Aerobic system requires oxygen to produce energy. It uses carbohydrates, fats, and proteins to produce ATP. Carbohydrates are the primary source of energy at the onset of exercise and during high-intensity work followed by fats during prolonged exercise of low to moderate intensity *(longer than 30 minutes)*

Energy Pathways

- *ATP (stored in muscles)*: 0-4 Seconds *(Strength and Power)*

- *ATP+PCr (Phosphagen)*: 0-10 seconds *(Sustained Power)* - *Immediate quick energy*

- *ATP+PCr+Lactic Acid* (Glycolytic): 0-90 seconds *(Anaerobic Power-Endurance)*

- *Aerobic Oxidation*: 90 seconds to 3+ minutes *(Aerobic Endurance)*

Any form of exercise can be broken down by two factors: *Intensity and Duration.* These two factors are inversely related. If the intensity is high the duration will be short and the lower the intensity the longer the duration. Think about *sprinting vs walking.* The ratio of intensity and duration of an exercise dictates the *predominant energy system* that is used. However, all of the energy systems are active and work together to provide energy for our bodies during exercise. They just alternate the workload of this energy production based on the demands placed on our body. *ATP-PC and anaerobic glycolysis* are the immediate systems, but the other systems are still active and a small portion of energy comes from them as well. *Aerobic oxidation* takes over as the predominant system for long-duration endurance activities.

Our bodies prefer aerobic or oxidative metabolism because *carbon dioxide and water* are more easily eliminated from our bodies than *lactic acid* which is produced by the anaerobic systems without oxygen.

Training Considerations

The initial stage of an exercise program should consist of low-intensity exercises for clients who are new to resistance training. When muscles are systematically stressed in a progressive manner, they gradually increase in size and strength. If they are stressed beyond normal demands, this can cause large-scale cell damage and *Delayed onset muscle soreness (DOMS)*. Progressing a client too quickly to higher intensity exercises could also cause injury, and reduce their adherence to regular exercise. Designing an exercise program that begins at a low level of intensity then gradually progresses intensity as the client physically and psychologically adapts to the training stress increases results and long-term exercise adherence.

The rate of development decreases as a person reaches their genetic potential for muscle size and strength. This is known as the *point of diminishing returns.* Variation in training becomes more important in this stage to continue seeing additional strength gains.

Training sessions should include the following three components:

> **Warm-up**: At least 5 – 10 minutes of low to moderate cardio and muscular endurance activities. The goal is to prime the body for movement and help reduce the chance of injury during the conditioning phase. Warm-ups also stimulate proprioception of the nervous system. *Dynamic stretching, bodyweight movements, elliptical, treadmill, or other cardio equipment.*

> **Conditioning**: At least 20 – 60 minutes of aerobic, resistance, neuromotor, and/or sports-specific activities.

> **Cool-down**: At least 5 – 10 minutes of low to moderate cardio and muscular endurance activities. The cool-down helps the body transition into the recovery process and gradually return the heart rate to baseline levels. *Stretching, bodyweight movements, decompressing from the workout.*

Excess Post Oxygen Consumption (EPOC) is the elevation of metabolism after exercise where our bodies consume more oxygen than resting levels for a short period of time after exercise. EPOC helps to restore our baseline levels of stored ATP for energy.

Recovery and adequate rest between training sessions ensure the body is recovered and functioning optimally. *Active rest along with self-myofascial release* can help ease any muscle tension from a previous training session.

Detraining or reversibility of conditioning refers to when the training stimulus is stopped the body gradually returns to its pre-conditioned state. It is a partial or complete reversal of the physiological adaptations gained through exercise. The phrase *"Use it or Lose it"* is a simple way to remember this concept.

Rhabdomyolysis: Often a sign of overtraining this condition happens when a rapid breakdown of muscle tissue results in the release of intramuscular proteins *(myoglobin, myosin protein)* into the bloodstream. This can be potentially harmful to the kidneys and could lead to kidney failure and sometimes death in extreme cases.

Valsalva maneuver: Moderate forceful exhalation against a closed airway while pressing out as if blowing up a balloon. The Valsalva maneuver is commonly used in powerlifting to stabilize the trunk during exercises like the squat and deadlift. The Valsalva maneuver should be avoided by the general population as it increases intra-abdominal pressure, blood pressure, and heart rate. This can be dangerous by hindering a person's cardiac output and cause dizziness or fainting.

Types of Training Programs

High-Intensity Interval Training (HIIT): Alternating brief periods of high-intensity activity followed by less-intense recovery periods. This type of training produces greater benefits in a shorter amount of *"training time."* Benefits include improved speed, endurance, recovery time, cardiovascular health, insulin sensitivity, fat burning, and increased metabolism. Interval training should not be performed on consecutive days to reduce the potential for overtraining. Typically performing HIIT on 2 – 3 non-consecutive days per week is sufficient.

*Interval training promotes greater improvements in VO$_2$ Max and lactate threshold enhancing a person's ability to sustain higher intensities of exercise for longer periods.

Steady-State Training: Involves activity without rest intervals. This type of training can be performed at low, moderate, or high intensities. Continuous training improves aerobic fitness, endurance, and aids in weight loss. This type of training is more time consuming than interval or circuit training and also does very little for anaerobic fitness.

Circuit Training: Involves performing several continuous exercises in a short period of time. This type of training induces metabolic and cardiovascular responses that could improve aerobic capacity. It also targets strength building and muscular endurance.

Super setting: Consecutive performance of two exercises either for the same or different muscle groups.

Olympic lifting: Total body resistance exercises that recruit most major muscle groups. Olympic lifts are the most complex exercises to perform but also are considered the most effective for increasing total-body power. The clean and jerk, snatch and overhead squats are some examples.

Variation in training: No one program should be used without changing the exercise stimulus over time.

Periodization

Periodization describes a division of a training program into smaller, progressive stages. It incorporates **Progressive Overload** and the **Principle of Specificity (SAID)** to vary the amount and type of stress placed on the body. This allows for adaptation while also allowing adequate rest and recuperation to prevent overtraining or injury. Periodization breaks training up into phases or cycles:

- ➤ **Macrocycle** = *Annual plan (6 – 12 months)*
- ➤ **Mesocycle** = *Monthly plan (1 – 3 months)*
- ➤ **Microcycle** = *Weekly plan (2 – 4 weeks)*

You will create a **training plan** to meet a client's goals, that details the form of training, length of time, future changes, and specific exercises to be performed. This sets the *expectations* for the client upfront along with realistic *timeframes for goal achievement*. It also provides them with a detailed *system to follow* to reach their *goals*.

Linear periodization: Classic or traditional strength and power programming that provides a consistent training protocol within each microcycle and changes the training variables after each microcycle. *(Strength training for one microcycle and power training for the next)*

Linear periodization is great to use for untrained clients as it progresses them systematically thru each phase ensuring proper adaptations are met before moving to the next phase. This helps to prevent the risk of injury and overtraining. A traditional linear periodization program contains the following four phases:

1) **Hypertrophy phase** (high volume, short rest periods)
2) **Strength / Power phase** (reduced volume but increased resistance and rest periods)
3) **Peaking phase** (low volume but high resistance and longer rest periods)
4) **Recovery phase** (low volume and low resistance)

Undulating Periodization (nonlinear): Allows for variation in the intensity and volume throughout a training program that provides changes in the acute variables of workouts to achieve different goals on a daily or weekly basis. A typical undulating program would follow a 14-day cycle, with three or four different workouts *(Stabilization on Monday, Strength on Wednesday, and Power on Friday)*

A specific example is provided in the *Apply What you Know section Tables 11-20 and 11-21 from pages 509 to 511 of the Exercise Professional's Guide to Personal Training.* It shows a sample protocol to take an individual from a 200 lb max bench press to a 250 lb max bench press.

Plyometric Training

Exercises that use quick, powerful movements involving an eccentric contraction immediately followed by an explosive concentric contraction. Plyometrics often involve *hopping, jumping, bounding* movements for the lower body and *throwing and explosive pushing movements* for the upper body. ***Plyometric training should range from 1 – 3 non-consecutive days per week with 48 – 72 hours of recovery between sessions.***

The body will only move within the ***range of speed that the nervous system has been programmed to allow***. This is accomplished by progressing a client appropriately through the ACE IFT Model. Plyometric training falls within the load/speed phase and works to improve *neuromuscular efficiency* and the ***range of speed*** set by the nervous system.

Think of it as increasing the speed and strength of communication from our nervous system to our muscular system. Like going from a dial-up internet connection to a high-speed fiber-optic connection. We are strengthening the signal which ***decreases our reaction time.***

Plyometric training enhances the *excitability, sensitivity, and reactivity* of the neuromuscular system. It also increases the following:

- ➢ **Rate of force production**: Ability of muscles to exert maximal force output in a minimal amount of time.
- ➢ **Motor unit recruitment**: The activation of the motor units in a successive manner to produce more strength.
- ➢ **Firing frequency**: The number of activation signals sent to a single motor unit in 1 second.
- ➢ **Motor unit synchronization**: The simultaneous recruitment of multiple motor units resulting in more muscle tissue contracting at the same time.

Plyometric training involves 3 phases known as the **Stretch-Shortening Cycle**:

1) **Eccentric** muscle contraction *(loading of the muscle / stretch of the agonist)*
2) **Amortization** *(brief isometric pause between phases / transition phase)*
3) **Concentric** muscle contraction *(release of stored energy / shortening of the agonist)*

A rapid eccentric muscle action stimulates the stretch reflex of the ***muscle spindles*** and stores this ***elastic energy,*** which increases the force produced during the subsequent concentric muscle action. ***It's like pulling a rubber band back and releasing the stored "elastic energy."*** If the concentric muscle action doesn't immediately follow the eccentric muscle action or if the eccentric phase is too long the stored *"elastic energy"* dissipates and is lost as heat, and the potentiating ability of the stretch reflex is lost.

You can see the effects of the stretch-shortening cycle by squatting down slowly and pausing before trying to jump vertically into the air vs a quicker lowering followed by a rapid contraction jumping upward like you would get a rebound in basketball.

Optimal landing mechanics, postural alignment, and proper technique should be emphasized during plyometric training. The main thing to watch for is the client's knees caving in, and ensuring they are properly aligned through the ankle, knee, and hip in the landing position. Good cues to use for landing are *"chest over the knees"* or *"nose over the toes."* Clients will also want to avoid landing flat-footed and look for their feet to land softly on the midfoot gradually reducing the speed before stabilizing in the landing position with ankles, knees, and hips flexed.

Encourage your clients to drop their hips and avoid locking their knees when landing. This will help them absorb the forces and develop the optimal glute dominance in the squat position. Plyometric exercise should also be performed early in a workout when the client is still fresh, they should not be performed once fatigue sets in. Example exercise progression listed below.

- Squat jump with stabilization
- Box jump up with stabilization
- Box jump down with stabilization
- Multiplanar jump with stabilization

Plyometric training protocols for the upper and lower body are covered from pages 495 – 500 of the Exercise Professional's Guide to Personal Training.

Speed, Agility, and Quickness Training (SAQ)

SAQ is beneficial for all individuals, not just athletes. Speed, Agility, and Quickness are valuable attributes that can be used in everyday life. Walking on uneven surfaces, moving out of harm's way, and moving to save a falling object or a person all require some level of SAQ to perform effectively. *SAQ training should range from 1 – 3 non-consecutive days per week with 48 – 72 hours of recovery between sessions.*

- ➢ **Speed** is the ability to move the body in one intended direction as fast as possible. Running speed is determined by stride rate and stride length.
    - ○ *Stride rate*: The number of strides taken in a given amount of time or distance.
    - ○ *Stride length*: The distance covered with each stride.
- ➢ **Agility**: The ability to maintain **center of gravity** over a changing **base of support** while changing direction at various speeds. Your ability to accelerate, decelerate, stabilize, and change direction quickly while maintaining posture and control.
- ➢ **Quickness (reaction time)**: The ability to react to a stimulus with an appropriate muscular response without hesitation. Ability to react and change body position with the maximal rate of force production during functional activities. *How quickly can your nervous system process input and elicit a response?*

Speed and Agility drills are shown in Tables 11-17 thru 11-19 from pages 503 – 507 of the Exercise Professional's Guide to Personal Training.

Flexibility describes the normal extensibility of soft tissue, which allows a joint to be moved through its full range of motion. Flexibility requires extensibility, which leads to a dynamic range of motion that requires neuromuscular efficiency.

- **Extensibility** is the capability of a muscle to be elongated or stretched.

- **Dynamic Range of Motion (ROM)** is the combination of flexibility and the nervous system's ability to control this range efficiently *(which describes neuromuscular efficiency)*.

- **Neuromuscular efficiency** is the ability of the neuromuscular system to allow agonists, antagonists, and stabilizers to work synergistically to produce *(concentric),* reduce *(eccentric),* and dynamically stabilize *(isometric)* the entire kinetic chain in all three planes of motion. ***It describes how coordinated and controlled a person is.***

When flexibility is limited, faulty movement patterns arise and are reinforced during exercise. Flexibility training ***improves communication between the nervous system and the muscular system.*** This is a crucial component of being able to move functionally. A good indicator of dynamic range of motion is to see if you can take a ***full breath at the end ranges of desired positions.*** If you can get into a position but lock-up holding your breath, and it's a struggle to maintain, then you do not have full end range control of that position.

A good test is to get down into a ***deep resting squat*** and feel how much control you have there. Below are some indicators of dynamic range of motion and owning a position.

- *Can you take a deep breath through your nose?*
- *Is your back straight, or are you rounding or reaching forward to maintain your balance?*
- *Are your feet straight, or turning out?*
- *Is the weight evenly distributed in your feet, or are you more on your toes or heels?*
- *Can you activate your glutes and core?*

Davis's law states that soft tissue models along the lines of stress.

Relative flexibility: The human movement system's way of finding the path of least resistance during movement.

It's funny to think about, but oftentimes we are trying to get our bodies to move more like we did as young children. Watch how toddlers move around and play. Their bodies are pliable and proprioceptive. There are no imbalances yet to cause faulty movement patterns. A toddler can easily play in a resting squat position for several minutes without thinking about it, or roll around and spring up and down off the floor with no problem. They are using proprioceptive input to control their ***center of gravity*** and changing ***base of support*** without being consciously aware of it.

Stretching Techniques

Static Stretching involves slowly move into the end range position then holding the stretch at the point of tightness for up to 30 seconds. Static stretching can be performed actively or passively.

> ➤ **Active stretching** involves adding additional force to increase the intensity of the stretch.

> ➤ **Passive stretching** is when the person stretching is not actively involved. The person assumes a position and then either holds it with another part of the body or with assistance from a partner or some other apparatus (resistance band or towel)

Proprioceptive Neuromuscular Facilitation (PNF) is a method of promoting the response of neuromuscular mechanisms *(autogenic inhibition and reciprocal inhibition)* This is done through the stimulation of proprioceptors in an attempt to gain more stretch in a muscle. PNF involves both stretching and contracting the targeted muscle group. There are 3 basic types of PNF stretching: *hold-relax, contract-relax, and hold relax with agonist contraction.* All 3 types begin with the personal trainer holding a passive pre-stretch for the client for 10 seconds.

> ➤ **Hold-Relax**: The client holds and resists the trainer creating an isometric contraction for a minimum of *6 seconds.* This is followed by a relaxation phase of the muscles for *30 seconds* in an assisted passive stretch from the personal trainer. This triggers an *autogenic inhibition response* that should increase the ROM in the target muscle group.

> ➤ **Contract-Relax**: The client pushes against the force generated by the trainer to create a concentric contraction through the full range of motion. This is followed by the same relaxation phase of the muscles for *30 seconds* in an assisted passive stretch from the personal trainer triggering an autogenic response and increased range of motion.

> ➤ **Hold-Relax with agonist contraction**: This technique is the same as the hold-relax but the opposing muscle group is concentrically contracted during the passive stretching portion. This adds to the ROM and stretch force by triggering both autogenic inhibition and reciprocal inhibition. This technique is considered the most effective.

*Activating your Glutes during a Hip flexor stretch will further inhibit the hip flexors and increase the stretch.

Dynamic Stretching describes moving parts of the body through a full ROM while gradually increasing the reach and/or speed of that movement. Progressing from smaller to larger ROM in a controlled manner. Dynamic stretching mimics a movement pattern to be used in the upcoming workout so they are great to use during warm-ups to prime the body for the conditioning segment. It prepares the neuromuscular systems for a more intense version of the movement.

Ballistic Stretching: Involves a bouncing type movement to reach the muscle's ROM limits. Ballistic stretching is generally not appropriate for the general population and mostly used by athletes who require ballistic type movements for their sport.

Self-Myofascial Release (SMR) focuses on the neural system and the fascial system. A foam roller or a lacrosse ball is used to break up tight areas and knots in the fascia to help release tension. The goal is to find tender or tight spots in the soft tissue *(muscles)*. Once found hold on this spot until the tenderness begins to decrease. This causes Golgi tendon organ (GTO) activity and decreases muscle spindle activity, thus triggering an autogenic inhibitory response.
A tender spot is defined as pain/discomfort classified as 6-9 from a 1-10 point scale.

Fascia: A strong web of connective tissue that wraps and surrounds muscle fibers, bones, nerves, and blood vessels. The myofascial system covers individual muscles as well as connecting groups of larger muscles together. It provides structural support and protection.

Common SMR form mistakes include the following:

- Rolling too quickly.
- Not identifying the tender spot.
- Not holding static pressure on the tender spot.
- Tensing the body in the presence of discomfort.
  Relax the muscle and focus on deep breathing.

Three types of stretching to improve ROM: *Static, Dynamic,* and *PNF.* Stretching should be done 2-3 days per week but is most effective when performed daily.

Stretching Tips

- Hold stretches for appropriate timeframes to allow for the inhibitory response and muscle relaxation caused by Golgi Tendon Organs (GTOs) muscle spindles.

- It's important to remind clients to continue to breathe during all stretching techniques and avoid holding their breath.

- Joints should never be taken past their normal range of motion while performing these various stretching techniques.

- Static stretching longer than 30 seconds prior to lifting or activities that requires maximal strength and power is not recommended as it can inhibit the muscle's ability to activate with maximal force.

Performing mostly dynamic and active stretching before sports activities or resistance training, saving the extended foam rolling and static stretching for after the workout to decompress or in the evening before bed. Static stretching and foam rolling can also be done at times when an individual is not planning to lift or perform. If static stretching is done prior to a training session, make sure to finish the warm-up with a quick activation of that same muscle group. For example, if a client is feeling tight in their low back or hamstrings before a workout, they could foam roll or static stretch for shorter holds and finish with some glute bridging to reactivate those muscles to contract. This will ensure they are no longer inhibited from the stretch.

Table 11-7 on page 484 of the Exercise Professional's Guide to Personal Training shows the FITT-VP recommendations for Flexibility Exercise.

Nutrition and Human Performance

Nutrition is the process by which a living organism assimilates food and uses it for the growth and repair of tissues.

There are 6 classes of nutrients: Carbohydrates, Fats, Protein, Vitamins, Minerals, and Water

Macronutrients: Carbohydrates, Fats, and Protein *These are the energy sources for our body*

> **Micronutrients:** Vitamins and Minerals
>
> - **Fat soluble nutrients:** Vitamins A, D, E, and K
>
> - **Water soluble nutrients:** Vitamins B, C, and Niacin
>
> - **Minerals:** Calcium, Phosphorus, Magnesium, Iron, Zinc, Copper, Selenium, Iodine, Fluoride, Chromium, Sodium, and Potassium

Vitamins and minerals should primarily come from eating a healthy diet with lots of vegetables, fruits, whole grains, dairy, and lean meats rather than relying on supplements such as a multivitamin to provide the recommended amounts.

Nutrient density describes the nutrient content of food relative to its calories.

There are **20 amino acids** found in the human body, **9 essential** and **11 non-essential**. The body cannot produce essential amino acids so they must be obtained from the foods we eat, whereas nonessential amino acids can be produced by the body.

Types of Fat

- **Long-chain:** Contains 14 or more carbon atoms
- **Medium-chain:** Contains 8-12 carbon atoms *Medium-chain triglycerides (MCT) are an excellent source of fuel for the body.*
- **Short-chain:** Contains 6 or fewer carbon atoms
- **Polyunsaturated:** Helps lower blood cholesterol levels
- **Monounsaturated:** Helps lower blood cholesterol levels while maintaining HDL
- **High-density lipoproteins (HDL):** Carry lipids away from storage into the liver for metabolism and /or excretion. They are considered *"good cholesterol"*
- **Low-density lipoproteins (LDL):** The major carrier of cholesterol and other lipids in the blood. They are often referred to as *"bad cholesterol"*

Consuming polyunsaturated and monounsaturated *"healthy fats"* along with regular exercise has been shown to improve lipid profiles. **Regular exercise also helps to reduce LDL cholesterol.**

Kilocalorie *(Calorie)* Breakdown

The actual definition of a calorie is a unit of heat energy required to raise the temperature of 1kg (liter) of water 1°C. In simple terms, ***Calories describe how much energy food sources have.***

- ➤ **Fat** = 9 calories per gram
- ➤ **Protein** = 4 calories per gram
- ➤ **Carbohydrates** = 4 calories per gram
- ➤ **Alcohol** = 7 calories per gram
- ➤ **3500 kcal** *(calories)* = 1 pound of fat

AMDR *(Acceptable Macronutrient Distribution Ranges)*

Carbohydrates: 45% - 65% of total calories

It is recommended that an individual consumes 6 – 10 grams of carbs per Kg of bodyweight. This equates to 2.7 to 4.5 grams per pound lb. The majority of all carbohydrate intake should come from complex carbohydrates *(veggies, sweet potatoes, whole grains)*

- ➤ A 180 lb person would fall in the range of ***486 – 810 grams of carbohydrates per day***. 1 gram of carbohydrates yields 4 calories so this would be ***1944 – 3240 calories per day.***

Protein: 10% - 35% of total calories

0.8 grams per kilogram of body weight per day is recommended for the general population. Adult athletes can range from 1.2 up to 2.0 g per kg of bodyweight depending on their amount of training and recovery needs.

- ➤ A 180 lb person would fall in the range of ***65 grams for the general population or 98 - 164 grams per day for an athlete.*** 1 gram of protein yields 4 calories so this would be ***260 calories per day for the general population or 392 – 656 calories per day for an athlete.***

Fats: 20% to 35% of total calories

- ➤ A 180 lb person would fall in the range of ***80 grams per day for an athlete.*** 1 gram of fat yields 9 calories so this would be around ***720 calories per day for this individual.***

Make sure you understand how to calculate macronutrient requirements based on your client's ***current weight and activity level.*** You need to be able to calculate based on ***calories per gram and the percentage of total recommended calories for each macronutrient.*** A good way to practice this is to track the food that you consume for one day and then calculate the percentages and grams of macronutrients based on your total intake. There is a great app for tracking food called ***MyFitnessPal.*** It allows you to scan barcodes on most food labels using a smartphone camera and it will automatically input the nutritional data. This is linked in the **Personal Trainer Resources blog → www.cptprep.com/single-post/resources**

Five Key Recommendations based on the Dietary Guidelines

1) **Follow a healthy eating pattern across the lifespan.** Including a variety of vegetables, fruit, grains, dairy, foods rich in protein sources, and limited amounts of saturated fats. If alcohol is consumed, it should be in moderation which is defined as up to one drink per day for women and two drinks per day for men. One drink is equivalent to one 12-ounce beer, 5 ounces of wine, or 1.5 ounces of hard liquor. The most important components of healthy eating patterns include high intakes of vegetables and fruits and low intakes of processed foods *(meats, sugar-sweetened beverages, and refined grains).*

2) **Focus on variety, nutrient density, and amount of foods consumed.** Nutrient-dense foods provide high levels of vitamins, minerals, and other nutrients that may have health benefits relative to caloric content *(vegetables, fruits, grains, dairy, protein foods (meats, poultry, eggs, nuts, and seeds, and oils)*

3) **Limit calories from added sugars and saturated fats, and reduce sodium intake.** Foods that are heavily processed or high in added sugars are often referred to as **"empty calorie"** foods as they supply little or no nutritional value. You can think of them as the opposite of **"nutrient-dense foods."** Added sugars mostly come from beverages, snacks, and sweets.

4) **Shift to healthier food and beverage choices.** *See Figure 6-11 on Page 182 of the Exercise Professional's Guide to Personal Training*

5) **Support Healthy Eating Patterns for All.** *See Figure 6-12 on Page 185 of the Exercise Professional's Guide to Personal Training which shows a Socio-Ecological Model about incorporating all sectors of society to make the US healthier.*

Dietary Reference Intakes (DRI)

➢ **Recommended Dietary Allowance (RDA)** level of intake of a nutrient that adequately meets the needs of all healthy people.

➢ **Estimated Average Requirement (EAR)** is the adequate intake in 50% of the age / sex-specific group of people. Consuming between the EAR and RDA means you likely have a sufficient amount of the desired nutrient.

➢ **Tolerable Upper Intake Level (UL)** This is the maximal limit that is unlikely to pose a risk to adverse health effects in most individuals.

➢ **Adequate Intake (AI)** This is the adequate amount that seems to be sufficient for good health based on research.

Keep in mind that these values are based on the normative data collected and that there could be outliers who could need different requirements based on their genetics or an underlying condition.

Fueling Before, During, and After Exercise

Pre-exercise goals are to optimize *glucose availability* and glycogen stores and *provide the fuel needed* to support exercise performance. *1 – 4.5 grams of carbs per kg of body weight is recommended with moderate protein, low fat, and approximately 400 – 800 calories total.*

During exercise, the goal is to sustain fuel *(glucose levels)* while staying hydrated. It should be noted that exercise lasting less than one hour *(which will be the majority of training sessions for most individuals)* can be adequately fueled with existing glucose and glycogen stores. However, when exercise lasts longer than one hour, blood glucose levels begin to decrease and after 1 – 3 hours of continuous exercise muscle glycogen stores may become depleted. To maintain fuel for longer-duration endurance-type exercise individuals should consume glucose-containing beverages and snacks such as sports drinks. *30 – 60 grams of carbs per hour of training is recommended. Consumed in 15 - 20-minute intervals)*

Post-exercise the main goal is to replenish glycogen stores and facilitate muscle repair. For most moderate-intensity exercise normal dietary practices following exercise will facilitate recovery within 24 – 48 hours. However, individuals who are training at higher intensities or multiple times per day, such as athletes can benefit from strategic refueling of mostly carbohydrates and moderate protein. *Refueling within 30 minutes after exercise, and then every two hours after for 4 – 6 hours before returning to normal eating routine.*

Fluid and Hydration Recommendations

> **Pre-exercise** drink 500 – 600 mL (17 – 20 oz) 2 hours prior to exercise
> **During exercise** drink 200 – 300 mL (7 – 10 oz) every 10 – 20 minutes during exercise or preferably, drink based on sweat losses.
> **Post-exercise** drink 450 – 675 mL for every 0.5 Kg of body weight lost or (16 – 24 oz) for every pound.

A good indicator of hydration is urine color. When optimally hydrated urine should be a near clear pale yellow, darker colored urine indicates a state of dehydration. Proper hydration during exercise produces the following benefits:

- A less pronounced increase in heart rate
- A less pronounced increase in core body temperature
- Improvement in cardiac stroke volume and cardiac output
- Improvement in skin blood flow *(enabling better sweat rates and improved cooling)*
- Maintenance of better blood volume
- A reduction in net muscle glycogen usage *(improving endurance)*

Ideally, clients should aim for a 1:1 fluid loss ratio consuming the same amount of fluid as they lost in sweat. A pre and post-exercise body weight is an easy way to assess post-exercise hydration needs. *Aim for no more than 2% loss in body weight. 180lb man would be at 3.6 lbs.*

Nutrition and Health

A lot of popular diet trends eliminate or restrict certain foods or macronutrients. However, there is strong scientific evidence that supports that it is not the relative proportion of macronutrients that determines long-term weight-loss, but whether the individual can maintain their energy balance of *calories consumed* and *calories burned.*

The goal of a dietary intervention to decrease weight is to create a caloric deficit so that the energy intake is less than the energy expended. *3,500 calories = 1 pound of fat* (bodyweight) so a *500 – 1,000 caloric deficit each day* leads to about *1 – 2 pounds of weight lost per week*. A combination of exercise *(energy expenditure)* and nutritional adjustments *(decreasing energy intake)* can be used for successful weight loss.

Regular physical activity provides health benefits regardless of body weight goals or how body weight changes over time. Regular exercise also helps to reduce abdominal fat and preserve lean body mass during weight loss efforts.

Glucose is a simple sugar that is the preferred energy source for the human body. It is a compound found in many carbohydrates. Some carbohydrates *(glucose)* are required for the oxidation *(burning)* of fat, and also help keep protein *(muscle tissue)* from being broken down. However, too much glucose *(carbs/sugar)* causes an excessive insulin response that encourages the production of fat. Any excess macronutrient will cause weight gain, but carbohydrates cause increases in glucose which if not utilized turns to body fat.

Glycemic index is a measure of how carbohydrates affect blood sugar levels. Low glycemic foods help maintain glucose *(blood sugar)* levels that in turn maintains insulin balance. This helps to keep the body out of the ***"fat-storing"*** state. **Glycogen** is the storage form of glucose that is found in the liver and muscle tissues. Blood glucose is generally at its highest one hour after eating, remains high for up to two hours, and then starts to fall.

Dietary fiber is a carbohydrate that cannot be digested, but aids in lowering fat and cholesterol absorption. Dietary fiber also improves blood sugar control. Since dietary fiber is non-digestible it is subtracted from the total carbohydrate amount of a given food. **If a food has 22 grams of total carbohydrates with 12 grams of dietary fiber then it has 10 grams of net carbs.*

The human body is *incapable of using protein for anabolic (tissue-building) purposes above the level of 1.5 grams per kilogram of body weight.* Overconsumption of protein above this amount is either burned as a source of energy or stored as fat. Excess protein also has to be excreted by the kidneys which can lead to increased metabolic waste and dehydration.

The NIH Body Weight Planner → www.niddk.nih.gov/bwp is a useful tool for setting safe weight loss, maintaining current weight, or increasing body weight over time.

Nutrition and Scope of Practice

Personal trainers can and should share general nonmedical nutritional information with their clients. A lot of clients may have misconceptions about nutrition. Sharing evidence-based dietary guidelines and resources help educate your clients about basic nutritional requirements. Sources such as ***Dietary Guidelines for Americans and MyPlate*** are recommended in the ACE Guide. Topics within the scope of practice include:

> *Principles of healthy nutrition and food preparation*

> *Food to be included in the balanced daily diet*

> *Essential nutrients needed by the body*

> *Actions of nutrients on the body*

> *Effects of deficiencies or excesses of nutrients*

> *How nutrient requirements vary through the lifecycle*

> *Principles of pre-and post-workout nutrition and hydration*

> *Information about nutrients contained in foods or supplements*

Teaching clients to effectively read nutrition labels and understand serving sizes along with calories and nutrients can be very beneficial. This can be a confusing task with the way foods are labeled and advertised today. ***Figure 6-13 on Page 190 of the Exercise Professional's Guide to Personal Training*** shows a great stepwise approach to explaining food labels to your clients.

In general, 5% of daily value is considered low and 20% of daily value is considered high. ***Ingredients are listed in order of abundance***. Ingredients that are listed first are the most abundant in the product. A lot of times towards the end of the ingredient list you will see the phrase ***"contains 2% or less of the following."*** Another important note is that ***"partially hydrogenated oils" is another term for trans fats.*** But if they are less than 0.5 grams then the manufacture is allowed to list trans fats as 0.

A **DRI Calculator** → https://www.nal.usda.gov/fnic/dri-calculator/ to determine recommended nutrient needs based on sex, age, height, weight, and activity level can be found at the following web address. It's very easy to use and helpful to get a general baseline of where an individual should be.

Remember, it is ***out of the scope of practice for personal trainers to provide nutritional assessments, counseling, meal plans, or recommend supplements to their clients.*** Clients should be referred to a registered dietician for these services.

ACE Position Statement on Nutrition Scope of Practice for Personal Trainers can be found on pages 165 a 166 of the Exercise Professional's Guide to Personal Training and on ACEfitness.org

Nutritional Supplements

Supplements are defined as a substance that completes or makes an addition to the daily dietary intake of food.

Fitness professionals should not provide guidance or advice in regards to the consumption of supplements by their clients. Supplements are not approved by the **Food and Drug Administration (FDA).** It's left up to the manufacturers who are making the supplements to ensure their products are safe and effective. The FDA will only investigate and take a supplement off the market if found to be unsafe after they become available.

The **FDA and NIH** are reputable sites to reference supplement information. Although you cannot recommend supplements to your clients, you can and should be prepared to discuss information about the safety and efficacy of supplements as well as their regulation. This will help keep your clients informed while staying within your scope of practice.

In general, supplementation is only recommended by a qualified healthcare professional if the individual does not meet all of their micronutrient requirements of vitamins and minerals through their diet alone. This can occur because of various reasons, *type of diet consumed, geographic location, underlying conditions, and genetics.*

For example, those who live in the northern hemisphere may not get adequate sunlight in the winter to produce enough vitamin D. Women who become pregnant are often put on a prenatal vitamin supplement to ensure their micronutrient levels are optimal as the baby develops, especially their folic acid, iron, and calcium.

The ACE Guide lists nutritional supplements with little to no evidence to support the efficacy and/or apparent safety which include the following.

- ➢ **Glutamine**
- ➢ **Arginine**
- ➢ **Carnitine**
- ➢ **Chronic use of Antioxidants**

Supplements with Strong Evidence to Support Efficacy and Apparent Safety

Creatine is involved in the supply of energy for muscular contraction. When creatine supplementation is combined with a strength-training program, it has been shown to increase muscle mass, strength, and anaerobic performance. ***The typical dosage is 5 grams per day. Some also suggest a loading phase of 20 grams per day for 5 – 7 days.*** Creatine has been widely studied and has been shown to be apparently safe for normal healthy individuals.

Caffeine acts as a stimulant that primarily affects the *central nervous system, heart, and skeletal muscles.* Evidence shows that caffeine is effective for aerobic and anaerobic exercise performance. It helps to increase work capacity, time to exhaustion, and can reduce perceived effort during endurance exercise. The most effective ergogenic response has been observed when the dosage of caffeine is ***about 3 to 6 mg per kg of body weight and is ingested 30 – 60 minutes before exercise.*** For a 180lb individual, this would be 245 – 490 mg of caffeine. 16 ounces or 2 cups of black coffee ranges from 200 to 350 mg of caffeine for perspective. Caffeine doses greater than 6 mg per kg of bodyweight generally show less performance benefit and have a higher risk of adverse side effects. ***There can be potential negative effects of caffeine that vary from individual to individual, especially with greater intakes.***

Post-exercise Carbohydrate ingestion Having some carbs post-workout can help to replenish glycogen stores in the muscles. It's an ideal time within 30 minutes after exercising when your blood is flowing and glycogen is depleted from exercise. It is recommended to consume ***1.2 grams of carbs per kg of body weight at 15 – 30-minute intervals once a workout has been completed.***

Protein Supplementation Whey and casein are some of the most popular protein supplements. Whey protein contains all of the ***essential amino acids*** with high levels of ***branch-chain amino acids***, vitamins, and minerals. Studies of whey protein have shown health benefits including increased muscle hypertrophy and muscular strength. Casein accounts for 70% to 80% of milk protein and provides a sustained slow release of amino acids into the bloodstream. Some studies suggest that combining both whey and casein protein offers the greatest muscular strength improvement following a 10-week intensive muscular training program. It's important to note that most American males already consume over the recommended daily amount of protein. However, when properly used protein supplementation may augment resistance-training adaptations.

Sodium Bicarbonate *(baking soda)* has been shown to improve recovery from intense exercise by increasing the muscle buffering capacity. ***Ingestion of 0.2 to 0.4 grams per kg with 1 liter of fluids 60 – 120 minutes pre-exercise is recommended.***

β-alanine is an amino acid found in foods such as fish and meat. It was reported that the performance of high-intensity exercise lasting between 60 and 240 seconds benefited from β-alanine supplementation. ***3 – 6 grams per day for 4 – 10 weeks is recommended with a maintenance dosage of 1.2 grams per day beyond that timeframe.***

Domain III: Program Modification and Progression

Monitor, evaluate, and modify programs to promote client adherence and ensure progress toward goals.

Principles of Behavior Change

Operant Conditioning is the process by which behaviors are influenced by their consequences.

Antecedents are *cues or stimuli* that precede behavior and often signal the likely consequences of the behavior. An example would be laying out training clothes for a morning workout before going to bed the night before. The overall goal for *stimulus control* is to make being physically active as convenient as possible.

Positive reinforcement increases the future occurrence of that behavior. **Extinction** occurs when the positive stimulus that once followed a behavior is removed decreasing the reoccurrence of that behavior.

Negative reinforcement can also increase the reoccurrence of an undesirable behavior if the client does not have accountability or consequences for that behavior *(showing up late, lack of effort, etc.)* Personal trainers should provide the appropriate amount of feedback, encouragement, and consequences to help clients maintain desired behaviors.

Decision making involves the ability to control a situation and choose the appropriate course of action. Effective decision-making skills give control back to the person involved and allow them to dictate the next steps to take. Personal trainers should continuously provide their clients with the knowledge that empowers them to take ownership and be successful on their own.

The Health Belief Model (HBM)

FEAR is a powerful motivator. A decision to change occurs when a perceived threat of a potential health problem, susceptibility to the potential health consequences, and the belief that making suggested behavioral changes will result in a decreased risk of those consequences. An example would be a sedentary person who has high blood pressure that decides to regularly exercise and eat better to decrease their blood pressure naturally. They must believe that making behavioral changes will decrease the health risk associated with high blood pressure.

Self-Determination Theory

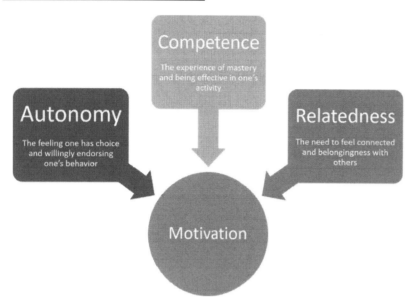

Competence: Relates to the self-perception that a person can successfully perform a task. When people feel that they have the skills needed for success, they are more likely to take actions that will help them achieve their goals. Competence is enhanced when they receive positive reinforcement or feedback.

Autonomy is the belief in free will, ***nobody likes being told what to do.*** People need to feel in control of their own behaviors and goals. This sense of being able to take action that will result in real change plays a major part in helping people feel self-determined.

Relatedness or Connection: People need to experience a sense of belonging and attachment to other people. This is part of our human hierarchy of needs.

*Intrinsic motivation is autonomous and Extrinsic motivation is controlled.
Intrinsic rewards are immediate, such as improved mood and relaxation that occurs after a workout, whereas extrinsic rewards are delayed such as wanting to lose 10 pounds.

Self-Esteem: Confidence in one's self-worth or abilities.

Self-Concept: Perceived worthiness, capabilities, and skills of one's self-based on inner belief and the responses of others.

Exercise environments can be perceived as ***Task-involving*** or ***Ego-involving***. Creating a caring, ***Task-involving*** environment that focuses on individual effort and improvement helps to increase ***self-esteem, competence, and autonomy.*** Whereas ego-involving climates can reduce self-esteem, increase anxiety, and cause physical exhaustion due to the competitive nature.

It's important to point out that some people thrive in competition and it can truly motivate them to be better and strive for excellence. However, the vast majority of people prefer task-involving environments.

Transtheoretical Model of Behavior Change

Examines an individual's *readiness to make a change.*

➤ **Stages of change**: Pre-contemplation, Contemplation, Preparation, Action, Maintenance
Know how to determine what stage of change a client is in based on their responses during motivational interviewing.

➤ **Process of change** involves using interventions specific to a client's current stage of change to help them transition to the next stage of change. This will help increase the success of the client adopting a new behavior. *"Meeting them where they are"*

➤ **Self-Efficacy**: The belief in one's capabilities to successfully engage in a physical-activity program along with one's ability for self-management, goal achievement, and effectiveness. **Self-Efficacy is developed through the following six sources of information**: *Past performance experience, Vicarious experience, Verbal persuasion, Physiological state appraisals, Emotional state and mood appraisals, and Imaginal experiences.*

➤ **Decisional Balance** involves the perceived pros and cons one has about adopting and/or maintaining an exercise program. In the early stages of pre-contemplation and contemplation, the perceived cons usually outnumber the pros. People in the later stages of action and maintenance perceive more pros than cons.

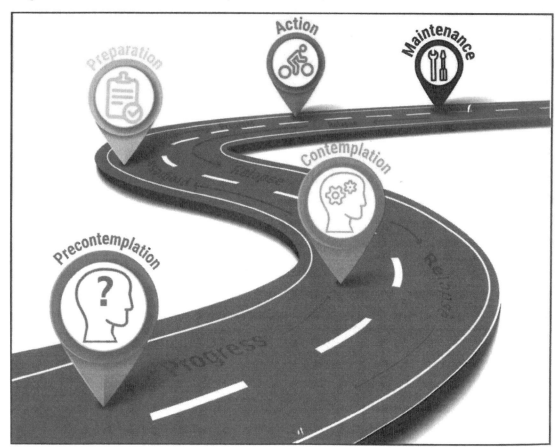

Stage 1: Precontemplation: People in this stage have no intention of changing. They do not exercise and do not intend to start in the next 6 months. The best strategy with pre-contemplators is education.

Stage 2: Contemplation: People in this stage do not exercise but are thinking about becoming more active in the next 6 months. The best strategy with contemplators is listening to them and providing education to help progress them to the next stage.

Stage 3: Preparation: People in this stage do exercise occasionally but are planning to begin exercising regularly in the next month. The best strategy in this stage is to help them clarify and set realistic goals and expectations. It's also helpful to implement the best time that works with their schedule and start building social support for exercise.

Stage 4: Action: People in the action stage have started to exercise but have not yet maintained the behavior of ***regular exercise for 6 months.*** It's important to discuss potential barriers to exercise to anticipate upcoming disruptions. Trainers should work with clients to help develop action steps for overcoming any barriers.

Stage 5: Maintenance: People in the maintenance stage have maintained change *(regular exercise)* ***for 6 months or more.*** People in this phase can still relapse so should have support and plans in place to stay on track for any potential disruptions.

Notice the common ***6-month benchmark*** that was used throughout the stages. Make sure you understand that a person who exercises but does not on a regular basis is considered to be in the Preparation stage, not the Action stage. The Action stage is when a person is exercising regularly for 6 months or less. The maintenance stage is when they have been exercising for 6 months or more.

This model also highlights the **importance of meeting your potential clients where they currently are *(both mentally and physically)*.** A good metaphor is when someone comes back down a hill during a race or hike to help another person. They ***meet them where they are*** and encourage them by climbing towards the goal together, instead of yelling encouragement from the top of the hill or finish line.

Assessing a Client's Stage with Open-ended Questions

> ➤ *What experience with physical activity have they had in the past?*
> ➤ *What worked best to help them stick to an exercise program?*
> ➤ *What worked the least? What contributed to their quitting an exercise program?*
> ➤ *During the last 6 months, what kept them from exercising?*
> ➤ *How did they keep up their exercise program when disruptions got in the way?*
>   *(Lack of time, Travel, Holidays)*

Client-Trainer Relationship

A client-trainer relationship is built upon **rapport, trust, and empathy**. Remember that **it's not about you**, each training session should be **client-centered.** You are there to provide excellent instruction on exercise technique and listen to the thoughts and concerns of your client. Think of yourself more as a **coach or mentor** rather than an authority figure on fitness. If you can do this in a **kind and genuine way**, you will **continually build trust and rapport** with your clients and increase your overall reputation as an excellent trainer. They will often tell others about you via word of mouth, and the cycle repeats.

There are four stages of the client-trainer relationship: Rapport Stage, Investigation Stage, Planning Stage, and Action Stage.

Rapport is defined as a relationship marked by mutual understanding and trust. This stage begins with the initial first impressions a client has and continues to develop through the use of excellent verbal and nonverbal communication. A personal trainer should possess excellent communication and teaching skills to create a climate of trust and respect with the client. Expressing **empathy, warmth, and genuineness** are three attributes to building a successful client-trainer relationship. People don't care how much you know until they know how much you care. Future teachings and valuable information that a personal trainer has to share will go unheard if they have not built this foundation of mutual understanding, trust, and respect with their clients. ***Positive first impressions are the foundation for the rapport-building process.***

The **Investigation** stage involves gathering information and demonstrating effective listening skills. Identifying client's readiness to change behavior; their current stage of behavioral change and personality style; collecting health and safety information; learning about lifestyle preferences, interests, and attitudes; understanding previous experiences, and conducting assessments. *A trainer should be able to identify the emotional needs behind the client's decision to start an exercise program and work with the client to address those needs.*

The **Planning** stage consists of the following steps: Setting goals, generating and discussing alternatives, formulating a plan, evaluating the exercise program, and designing motivation and adherence strategies.

The **Action** stage is where the exercise program begins. Implementing all of the programming components and providing instruction, demonstration, and execution of the program; implementing strategies to improve motivation and promote long-term adherence; providing feedback and evaluation; making necessary adjustments to the program; and monitoring the overall client experience and progression towards goals.

Types of Goals

> **Objective goal**: Something an individual is trying to accomplish; the object or aim of an action.

> **Subjective goal**: Goal based on experience or expectations; less tangible than an objective goal. *The continual aim for the type of person you wish to become, the principles you live by.*

> **Performance goal** is something achieved, such as being able to *run a 5k in 25 minutes.*

> A **Process goal** is something a client does *(the process)*, such as completing a certain number of workouts each week.

> An **Outcome goal** is something that is achieved externally such as weight loss or an increase in strength.

> **Long-term goals** should be set during the initial sessions with clients. A large goal is set to be achieved over a long period of time. *Usually made up of a series of smaller short-term goals.* Long-term goals should **align with the client's values** based on **who they want to be** and **what is important to them.** Goal commitment is increased when a client is involved in the goal setting process *(when they make their own goals)* or embrace the input from the fitness professional to help create them.

> **Short-term goal**: A goal that is set to be achieved within the near future. *Should be process-oriented and work towards achieving a long-term outcome goal.*

SMART Goals: Specific, Measurable, Attainable, Realistic, Timely *(Time-Bound)*

For example, saying **"I want to lose weight before my vacation this summer."** isn't specific or measurable, or saying **"I want to be strong enough to perform an unassisted pull-up."** isn't time-bound. However, saying **"I want to lose 10 pounds before my wedding in 3 months."** meets all of the criteria of a SMART goal.

Goal-Setting Theory: The following four mechanisms play a role in goal-related behavior change:

> **Directed attention**: Goals direct attention toward desired behaviors
> **Mobilized effort**: Goals lead to greater effort
> **Persistence**: Goals extend the time and energy devoted to the desired behavior
> **Strategy**: Goals increase the use of goal-relevant skills

A *goal* is a form of what someone *wants*. All human beings have wants and needs. It's our job as trainers to help clients *achieve what they want,* while also *addressing their needs* along the way. One way is to address their wants during the training session and their needs during the warm-up, cool-down, and off training days.

Emphasize Systems to Help Achieve Goals

The important question to ask after a goal has been set is, *"What system to put in place to achieve it?"* Clients can then focus on the system and ***process*** instead of looking for continual motivation to get there. Once laid out, the system can be followed even when motivation is low. This is often what separates those who achieve their goals and those who do not. The repetition of ***consistently*** repeating a behavior ***builds compound gains.***

In his book, ***Atomic Habits James Clear*** gives a great analogy of melting an ice cube. If you raise the temperature from 22°F to 31°F there will still be an ice cube. It looks like there is no change, it's not until you reach 32°F that the ice begins to melt. Progress is being made it's just happening ***below the surface of tangible measurement.***

Clients can get discouraged if they do not see progress, so it's important to be able to track progress and have ***small wins and rewards along the way.*** Helping clients focus on their ***intrinsic feelings and progress*** during an exercise program can boost their motivation. These feelings are ***immediate***. Improvements in mood, feeling more energetic and less stressed, and getting better sleep are all great internal fitness indicators of progress.

It's helpful to ask clients ***"What their plan is once their long-term goal has been achieved?"*** This can spark an open discussion on lasting lifestyle change and help them view exercise as an important component of a healthy life regardless of specific goals that are set. Learning to embrace the process and the intrinsic feelings associated with ***consistent healthy habits*** early in a training program can help with long term adherence.

Communication and Teaching Techniques

Listen: Active listening involves nodding, making eye contact, and restating important information the client has stated. Be non-judgmental and open-minded. Give verbal and nonverbal feedback to indicate attention and understanding. Make sure to receive affirmation from the client on feedback given. Identify statements that indicate a teaching and/or learning opportunity.

Empathize: Match the client's emotions to show affective empathy. The ability to identify with their perspective shows an understanding that helps to develop trust and rapport.

Positive Affirmation: Positive words promote positive attitudes and positive outcomes. Positive reinforcement and encouragement help the client to build self-esteem and motivation for exercise.

Intrinsic Motivation: Participation in exercise to achieve internal outcomes such as enjoyment of exercise itself or the sense of accomplishment after the workout is completed. Intrinsic motivation for exercise is better for lifelong adherence to exercise.

Extrinsic Motivation: Participation in exercise to achieve external outcomes such as weight loss and appearance. External motivation from the trainer should inspire intrinsic motivation of the client.

Motivational Interviewing *(ABC Approach)*: Helps a client commit to changing unhealthy behavior by combining empathetic counseling and a direct approach to decisive change. Ask open-ended questions that require more than a *"yes"* or *"no"* answer. Encourage the client to talk about what needs to be changed and then help them find ways to elicit that behavior change. Personal trainers should empower their clients to take control, be independent, and self-sufficient with their exercise program by teaching and helping them find enjoyment in the experience. Helping clients take ownership and control increases their intrinsic motivation. A personal trainer should not try to control or manipulate a client into acting a certain way as this will diminish the intrinsic motivation of the client.

> *"Nobody cares how much you know, until they know how much you care."*
> ~ Theodore Roosevelt

> *"Seek first to understand, and then to be understood."*
> If you are a good listener you build trust, then your client becomes open to your ideas.

> *"Without involvement, there is no commitment."*
> This is about adherence. If the client is not involved in making their program, they are far less likely to adhere to it.
> ~ Stephen Covey

Types of Learners

> **Visual**: Someone who learns through seeing images and techniques. Visual learners must first see what they are expected to know.

> **Auditory**: A person who learns best through listening. They depend on hearing and speaking as a primary way of learning.

> **Kinesthetic**: This learning style requires that you manipulate or touch material to learn. It is often combined with auditory or visual learning techniques producing multi-sensory learning.

"Tell, Show, Do" *Tell me and I'll forget, Show me and I may remember, Involve me and I'll understand.*

Trainers should keep this proverb in mind when teaching exercises to clients. Using a combination of *"Tell, Show, Do"* is the best practice when teaching. Starting with a brief and simple explanation *"Tell"* along with demonstration *"Show"* followed by the client performing the exercise *"Do."* The personal trainer should observe the client while they perform the exercise and prepare to provide helpful feedback.

Stages of Learning

> **Cognitive**

> **Associative**

> **Autonomous**

As clients try to understand a new skill they are in the initial *Cognitive* stage of learning. In the *Associative* stage of learning, clients begin to master the basics and are ready for specific feedback that will help them refine the motor skill. Clients are then performing motor skills effectively and naturally in the final *Autonomous* stage of learning. Our job as personal trainers is to provide just enough feedback to help our clients master the skill. Be careful not to overwhelm them with too much feedback, especially in the cognitive stage of learning. Small tips go a long way. Remember to *frame feedback in a positive way* pointing out what the clients should do rather than what they are doing wrong.

Client Feedback

Seeking client feedback will help ensure client satisfaction and enjoyment of the program. Paying attention to both verbal and nonverbal feedback will assist in properly progressing and modifying the client's training program as needed. Scheduling periodic program evaluations and goal reviews will also ensure that client expectations are met.

Effective Teaching Techniques

Motor Learning is the process of acquiring and improving motor skills with *practice and experience* which leads to relatively permanent changes in the body's capacity to produce skilled movements.

Think of the phrase *"Like riding a bike."* Once you know how to ride a bike it's hard to unlearn that skill. You can go years without riding one while still having the capability to ride with minimal mental effort.

This is also why *drilling* is so important in sport and skill development. The act of drilling or repeating the same skill or movement pattern over and over downloads that pattern into our system so that we can perform it with less mental effort.

Intrinsic and extrinsic feedback is used during the motor learning process.

Internal feedback refers to how our bodies feel internally during the movement *(which muscles are engaged, how much effort is being used)*

External feedback is information provided by an external source such as a personal trainer or mirror. External feedback should accomplish the following:

- Reinforce what is done well
- Correct errors if necessary
- Motivate clients to continue practicing and improving

The goal of *external feedback* is to get the client to *intuitively "feel"* when they are performing the exercise with proper technique. In the beginning stages of motor learning more external feedback is needed but as they master the skill they will be able to mostly rely on their *internal feedback* to perform the exercise.

Types of Feedback

➤ **Evaluative**: A summary for the client of how well they have performed a given task. *"You maintained great form and control during that set."*

➤ **Supportive**: Encourage the client when they perform a task properly. This type of feedback is motivational for the client and helps them adhere to the exercise program. *"Great job on that last set! Way to finish strong!"*

➤ **Descriptive**: Specific information that helps the client understand what they need to do in order to improve. *"Make sure to keep your core engaged and back straight during the deadlift, hinge at the hips."*

The type of feedback that provides information on progress can be referred to as *knowledge of results*.

Adherence to Exercise

- ➢ It takes about **6 months of regular exercise** to see lasting health benefits.
- ➢ 50% of people who begin an exercise program **quit within 6 months.**
- ➢ Involving clients in the planning stage of an exercise program by asking for their input and working together to design the program helps them take responsibility for the program and **increases exercise adherence.**
- ➢ An individual who perceives that the **benefits of exercise outweigh the barriers** to exercise is more likely to adhere to an exercise program.
- ➢ Helping clients achieve their own **self-regulation** for exercise is necessary to increase exercise adherence. Self-regulation strategies include planning exercise, setting exercise-related goals, self-monitoring exercise behavior, and avoiding relapse.

Overcoming Barriers

Factors influencing exercise participation and adherence: Personal Attributes *(Demographic Variables, Health Status, Activity History, Psychological Traits, Knowledge, Attitudes, and Beliefs)* Environmental Factors *(Access to Facilities, Time, and Social Support)* Physical-Activity Factors *(Intensity and Injury)*

Personal Barriers: These can be internal or behavioral such as lack of time, motivation, knowledge, injury, and extrinsic motivation. Discussing strategies for time management, sharing information about the benefits of exercise, and setting challenging but attainable goals can help increase a client's self-efficacy to overcome personal barriers.

Social Barriers: These barriers arise from within the client's social network *(close family and friends).* Examples of social barriers include caregiving *(such as child care),* lack of social support, and sociocultural barriers. Understanding what types of social support a client needs and teaching them how to obtain that support may help them achieve the support required to adhere to exercise. Social support has four types: *Emotional, Tangible, Informational, and Appraisal*

Environmental Barriers: These are physical barriers that are often outside of an individual's control that prevent them from being active. Lack of access to exercise facilities, bad weather, and safety concerns *(absence of sidewalks or bike lanes, crime)* are some examples. Providing clients with opportunities to be active outside of the gym, at their homes, or within their daily lifestyles can help overcome lack of access.

Avoiding Relapse: Psychological factors and high-risk situations such as life events *(births, deaths in the family),* holidays, injuries, decreased social support, and decreased motivation can impact continued adherence to exercise. These may cause a lapse *(a brief period of two or more weeks)* or relapse *(complete return to sedentary behavior)* in exercise adherence. Discussing potential relapse situations before they occur with a client can prepare them to overcome and maintain their exercise routine. **Assertiveness** is an important characteristic for achieving success and avoiding relapse. The more assertive clients are with regard to their progress, concerns, accomplishments, and struggles the more likely they are to achieve long-term success. Continuing self-regulation, intrinsic motivation along with setting achievable goals will help a client's self-efficacy, and prevention of relapse.

Chronic Disease Exercise Recommendations

Includes clients with the following health conditions or special needs:

- Coronary artery disease (CAD)
- Hypertension
- Stroke
- Peripheral arterial disease (PAD)
- Dyslipidemia
- Diabetes
- Metabolic syndrome
- Asthma
- Cancer
- Osteoporosis
- Arthritis

Clients with one or more of the conditions above should engage in a low to moderate intensity *individualized exercise program* designed for their specific needs. This will be based on their current health status, physical condition, and other factors identified in the screening process. The same principles described for the general population in the *ACE Integrated Fitness Training Model* can be followed, with *certain modifications when warranted.* Based on the following factors:

- Characteristics of the disease
- Any restrictions that the disease places on clients and how they will respond to exercise
- Disease severity
- Safety concerns
- Activities to emphasize
- Activities to avoid *(contraindications)*

You will often work with other *allied healthcare professionals* for clients with chronic diseases, especially if medical clearance is needed to participate in regular exercise. Ensure that you maintain close communication with the client's healthcare professionals and expand your knowledge in the applicable areas. Working as a team with *open communication is key to program success.*

The stress of having one or more chronic diseases can affect an individual's wellness both physically and emotionally. Oftentimes people with chronic issues identify themselves by the diagnosis. Stating *"I am diabetic"* rather than saying *"I have diabetes"* is an example. Helping our clients *separate the signs and symptoms of the disease from their sense of self-identity* can dramatically change their perspective in a positive way. Lifestyle is the most influential factor in the incidence of chronic diseases, even for those with genetic predispositions. Therefore, focusing on the *controllable lifestyle factors* of *regular activity, healthy eating, quality sleep, and recovery* can improve health outcomes and ease some of the mental stress related to the disease.

Considerations for Working with Clients with a Chronic Disease

➢ The overall goal with the majority of chronic health conditions is to preserve and improve the individual's functional capacity, help to mitigate treatable symptoms, and slow the aging processes involved with muscle loss, coordination loss, and bone density loss.

➢ Most people with a chronic health condition will not advance to the power phase and perform plyometrics.

➢ Seated and standing exercises are preferred over supine or prone.

➢ Clients with chronic health conditions should be thoroughly assessed prior to beginning an exercise program and have medical clearance if warranted. Oftentimes clients may have one or more of these chronic conditions.

➢ Contraindicated movements and exercises should be determined upfront before training begins.

➢ Understand your scope of practice when working with special populations and refer and communicate with your client's physician regularly. Remember as a fitness professional you are not qualified to diagnose or treat medical conditions and should work within the recommended guidelines set by the client's physician.

Coronary Artery Disease (CAD) is characterized by a narrowing of the coronary arteries that supply the heart muscle with blood and oxygen. The number one cause of death in the US is cardiovascular disease (CVD). The *American Heart Association* estimates that ***121.5 million Americans have one or more types of cardiovascular disorders***, including dyslipidemia *(high cholesterol)*, CAD, congestive heart failure, hypertension, stroke, and peripheral arterial disease (PAD). Well established risk factors of CVD include ***family history (genetics), hypertension (high blood pressure), diabetes, age, dyslipidemia, and lifestyle (poor diet, physical inactivity, and smoking).***

Moderate amounts of physical activity are associated with a 20% lower risk, where higher amounts have a ***30% or greater reduction in the risk of developing CAD.*** Diet and nutrition also play a factor. One study estimated that ***45% of US deaths caused by heart disease, stroke, and type 2 diabetes were attributable to dietary habits.***

Exercise should not continue if any of the following signs or symptoms are observed: ***Angina (chest pain), dyspnea (shortness of breath), lightheadedness or dizziness, pallor (pale skin), or rapid heart rate above established targets.*** Personal trainers should question their clients and be aware of such signs or symptoms before, during, and immediately after each exercise session. Make sure clients can recognize these signs and symptoms as well. If symptoms are present and persist, the emergency medical system should be activated and the client's physician should be notified.

Table 13-1 on page 599 of the Exercise Professional's Guide to Personal Training gives exercise guidelines for those with Cardiovascular Disease.

Hypertension describes an elevation in normal blood pressure. There are two types of hypertension. ***Primary hypertension*** is when there is no known or evident cause. This makes up ***90 – 95%*** of those with hypertension. ***Secondary hypertension*** makes up the other ***5 – 10%*** which can be attributed to an underlying cause such as kidney disease. It is estimated that ***103 million Americans have hypertension, which is about 1 in 3 people.*** The majority of people can treat their high blood pressure with lifestyle changes instead of medication, especially those with elevated or Stage 1 hypertension. The goal is to manage hypertension when it is present and prevent it through living a healthy lifestyle. This includes physical activity and eating a sensible balanced diet.

Categories of Blood Pressure in Adults *(measured in millimeters of mercury)*		
Category	*Systolic Blood Pressure*	*Diastolic Blood Pressure*
Normal	< 120 mmHg	< 80 mmHg
Elevated	120 – 129 mmHg	< 80 mmHg
Hypertension		
Stage 1	130 – 139 mmHg	80 – 89 mmHg
Stage 2	≥ 140 mmHg	≥ 90 mmHg

Risk factors for hypertension include ***stress, body weight (especially excess body fat), sleep, age, excessive sodium intake, increased alcohol intake, and physical inactivity.*** Notice that these are all modifiable risk factors. Even for those who are genetically predisposed to hypertension due to family history. ***Our genes respond to the inputs we give them.*** Just because we are predisposed to certain things doesn't mean they are inevitable. Most diseases, especially common diseases, are a combination of genetic risk and the environment. The good news is the environmental factors are controllable and seem to have a bigger influence on our overall health.

Considerations when working with clients with Hypertension:

- Avoid performing *isometric* exercises, inverted positions, and the ***Valsalva maneuver*** because they can dramatically raise blood pressure and associated work of the heart.

- Many hypertensive clients will be on medication for the condition and some medications such as beta-blockers and calcium channel blockers can alter the heart-rate response during exercise. Clients on these medications should be taught to use the talk test and RPE scale to monitor exercise intensity.

- Diuretic medications are also used to control blood pressure and special attention to hydration is needed for clients on these medications to avoid dehydration, especially in warm environments.

Table 13-4 on page 604 of the Exercise Professional's Guide to Personal Training gives exercise guidelines for those with Hypertension.

Stroke: A sudden and often severe attack due to blockage of blood flow or bleeding in the brain. Strokes are the second leading cause of death globally and the number-one cause of disability. The following are warning signs of a stroke that personal trainers should be aware of:

➢ **Walk**: Is their balance off? *(walking problems, dizziness, or loss of coordination)*

➢ **Talk**: Is their speech slurred or face droopy? *(confusion, trouble speaking or understanding others)*

➢ **Reach**: Is one side weak or numb? *(numbness or weakness of the face, arms, or legs)*

➢ **See**: Is their vision all or partially lost? *(trouble seeing in one or both eyes)*

➢ **Feel**: Does the client have a severe headache with no known cause?

Table 13-5 on page 607 of the Exercise Professional's Guide to Personal Training gives exercise guidelines for those recovering from a stroke.

Peripheral Arterial Disease (PAD) is a condition in which blood flow to the lower extremities is reduced due to the narrowing of arteries.

Intermittent Claudication is the manifestation of the symptoms caused by peripheral arterial disease that includes ***limping, lameness, or pain in the lower leg during mild exercise*** resulting from a decrease in blood supply to the lower extremities.

It's often hard to differentiate between intermittent claudication pain in the lower leg and a cramp or tightness in a deconditioned client. If their pain persists during exercise refer them to their physician immediately. Clearance is needed for any clients diagnosed with peripheral arterial disease as it is commonly associated with other chronic conditions like diabetes and coronary heart disease. The most prominent ***risk factors are smoking and diabetes.***

Before starting an exercise program people with PAD should have medical evaluation and clearance. Exercise guidelines should also be provided by the evaluating physician. To improve exercise capacity, clients should walk to the point of pain, followed by rest until the pain subsides, and repeat. If a client shows any symptoms of cardiovascular disease then exercise should stop and further evaluation is warranted before continuing an exercise program.

Table 13-6 on page 610 of the Exercise Professional's Guide to Personal Training gives exercise guidelines for those with PAD.

Dyslipidemia describes elevated lipid levels of LDL and total cholesterol. Dyslipidemia is best managed and improved by combining exercise with dietary changes that reduce body fat and weight.

Cholesterol is essential for life, it helps cell function, the production of hormones, vitamin D, and assists with fat digestion. However, undesirable levels are associated with atherosclerosis and the development of cardiovascular disease.

➢ **High-Density Lipoproteins (HDL)**: Carry lipids away from storage into the liver for metabolism and /or excretion. HDL makes up 20 – 30% of the body's total cholesterol. HDL is considered *"good cholesterol."* *The higher the HDL the lower the risk of CAD.*

➢ **Low-Density Lipoproteins (LDL)**: The major carrier of cholesterol and other lipids in the blood. Makes up 60 – 70% of the body's total cholesterol. LDL is typically referred to as the *"bad cholesterol"* because in excess it can accumulate on artery walls.

Value *(mg / dL)*	Classification
LDL Cholesterol	
< 100	Optimal
100 – 129	Near or above optimal
130 – 159	Borderline high
160 – 189	High
≥ 190	Very High
HDL Cholesterol	
< 40	Low
≥ 60	High
Total Cholesterol	
< 200	Desirable
200 – 239	Borderline high
≥ 240	High
Triglycerides	
< 150	Normal
150 – 199	Borderline high
200 – 499	High
≥ 500	Very High

One study showed that cardiorespiratory exercise combined with weight loss significantly *reduced total cholesterol and LDL "bad cholesterol" while raising HDL "good cholesterol."*

Moderate to vigorous intensity at higher frequencies and duration seem to be the most effective for improving HDL as they tap into the oxidative fat burning energy systems for fuel.

Table 13-9 on page 614 of the Exercise Professional's Guide to Personal Training gives exercise guidelines for those with Dyslipidemia.

Diabetes is a group of metabolic disorders involving an absolute or relative insufficiency of insulin secretion. Worldwide diabetes causes *more than 3.2 million deaths per year.* The primary treatment goals for diabetes are to normalize glucose metabolism and prevent diabetes-associated complications and disease progression.

Blood glucose is utilized by the muscles during exercise so this reduces the circulating blood glucose and insulin requirements. It also improves glucose tolerance and insulin sensitivity to allow the body to utilize the insulin that is produced to help maintain glucose levels.

> **Type 1** diabetes is a genetic form of diabetes where the body doesn't produce enough insulin *(which regulates blood sugar / glucose).* Individuals with this type of diabetes need insulin injections to help regulate their blood glucose. Type 1 diabetes is less common and makes up 5 – 10% of people with diabetes.

> **Type 2** diabetes makes up *more than 90% of those with diabetes.* As of 2018, about 21 million people have Type 2 diabetes in the US. This form of diabetes occurs when the body cannot respond normally to the insulin that is made. Type 2 diabetes is *strongly associated with obesity, especially abdominal obesity.* This causes insulin resistance and an increase in blood glucose.

Comparison of Type 1 and Type 2 Diabetes		
Characteristics	*Type 1*	*Type 2*
Age of onset	Usually < 35 years	Usually > 40 years
Clinical onset	Abrupt	Gradual
Family history	Not always	Yes
Body composition	Normal or thin	Usually obese *(central type)*
Blood insulin levels	Reduced or absent	Normal or increased
Cell insulin resistance	Absent or minor	Present
Treatment for control of hyperglycemia	Insulin, diet, and/or exercise	Weight loss, diet, oral hypoglycemic drugs, or insulin

If clients with type 1 diabetes or type 2 who need insulin do not have optimal levels of circulating glucose prior to exercise, their glucose levels can drop causing *hypoglycemia (low blood sugar)*. This drop can cause *weakness, dizziness, and fainting.* Be aware of these signs and symptoms during training. It is advised to check their glucose levels prior, during, and after exercise to make sure glucose levels are adequate. Glucose can be increased by eating simple carbohydrates *(juice, raisins, white bread)*. Insulin can also be regulated to help maintain glucose levels.

Diabetes Continued...

A 5% to 7% decrease in body weight can reverse insulin resistance. Although this decrease may not be an ideal body weight for those with obesity, it seems to reduce systemic inflammation enough to allow their bodies to begin utilizing the insulin that is produced. In other words, it's a step in the right direction for controlling diabetes and should be viewed as a positive achievement towards the goal of a healthier lifestyle.

Genetic factors also play a role in diabetes. However, genes are triggered by a combination of factors that are mostly related to lifestyle. Being *inactive, eating poorly, gaining weight, being exposed to pollutants, and stress* are some common factors.

Our lifestyles dictate our gene expression. If we signal them with positive inputs through a *healthy diet, exercise, and quality sleep* we can help mitigate some of the genetic predispositions we may have. Being active and eating more fiber are likely the two most important changes a person can make to lower systemic inflammation and the risk of developing metabolic diseases. A good rule of thumb is to try not to go more than two days without exercising.

It should also be noted that carbohydrates have the biggest impact on circulating blood glucose because they are quickly converted to blood sugar *(glucose)* once consumed. Especially simple carbohydrates *(sugary drinks, white pasta, and bread).* Complex carbohydrates also turn to blood glucose but do so more slowly because they have to be broken down further to utilize.

Blood glucose is generally at its highest one hour after eating, remains high for up to two hours, and then starts to fall.

Any excess macronutrient will cause weight gain but carbohydrates cause increases in glucose which if not utilized turns to body fat.

Proper footwear is essential for clients with diabetes or PVD to prevent constriction, ulcers, or injury due to *"peripheral neuropathy,"* which causes loss of sensation in the extremities.

Table 13-11 on page 618 of the Exercise Professional's Guide to Personal Training gives exercise guidelines for those with Diabetes.

Metabolic Syndrome (MetS) is a cluster of three or more of the following conditions:

- **Elevated waist circumference** *(≥40" for men and ≥35" for women)*
- **Elevated triglycerides** *(≥150 mg/dL)*
- **Reduced HDL cholesterol** *(<40 mg/dL for men and <50 mg/dL for women)*
- **Elevated blood pressure** *(≥130/85 mmHg)*
- **Elevated fasting blood glucose** *(≥100 mg/dL)*

The presence of metabolic syndrome increases a person's risk for developing *heart disease, type 2 diabetes, and stroke.* The primary treatment objective for metabolic syndrome is to reduce the risks through lifestyle interventions such as *healthy eating, increased physical activity, weight loss, and tobacco cessation.*

Table 13-12 on page 621 of the Exercise Professional's Guide to Personal Training gives exercise guidelines for those with Metabolic Syndrome.

The ACE Guide also has a case study for an initial consultation with a client who has multiple chronic diseases using the ABC Approach. These are helpful to give a framework on how to approach these common situations.

Chronic Obstructive Pulmonary Disease (COPD) describes chronic airway inflammation due to exposure to substances such as tobacco smoke and various other environmental and occupational pollutants. The three most common obstructive diseases are *asthma, chronic bronchitis, and emphysema.*

Asthma is a chronic inflammatory disorder of the airways that causes recurrent episodes of wheezing, breathlessness, chest tightness and coughing, particularly at night or in the early morning. ***Approximately 80% of people with asthma experience attacks during and/or after exercise.*** This is referred to as ***Exercise-induced bronchoconstriction (EIB).*** However, exercise conditioning can reduce the ventilatory requirement for various tasks making it easier for asthmatic individuals to perform daily activities and sports as well as reduce the severity of exercise-induced asthma (EIA) attacks.

Table 13-13 on page 627 of the Exercise Professional's Guide to Personal Training gives exercise guidelines for those with Asthma. Most people with controlled asthma will benefit from regular exercise and can follow guidelines for the general population.

Chronic bronchitis describes excessive production of sputum, often resulting in airflow obstruction.

Emphysema is characterized by distention and destruction of the alveoli *(tiny air sacs in the lungs)* causing airway narrowing and reduced ventilation.

Table 13-14 on page 628 of the Exercise Professional's Guide to Personal Training gives exercise guidelines for these conditions.

Cancer is a type of disease where cells in the body grow out of control, divide, and invade other tissues. It describes a collection of approximately 200 related diseases. Cancer develops when the DNA of normal cells is damaged. Cancer is the second leading cause of morbidity and mortality worldwide. The cause of cancer is complex and linked to many factors that are both environmental and lifestyle-related. There are five leading behavioral and dietary risks.

1. **High BMI** *(being overweight)*
2. **Low consumption of fruits and vegetables**
3. **Physical inactivity**
4. **Tobacco use**
5. **Alcohol intake**

The goal of exercise in the treatment of cancer is to help enhance one's overall quality of life thru cardiovascular conditioning, preventing musculoskeletal deterioration *(atrophy),* reducing symptoms such as nausea and fatigue, and improving the client's mental health.

Regular physical activity plays a significant role in improving risk factors associated with cancer development. Exercise can help to maintain a healthy body weight as well as regulate hormonal and immune function, which likely helps to mitigate some of the risks of developing cancer in the first place. Exercise also helps to reduce common side effects of cancer treatment including *anxiety, depressive symptoms, fatigue, physical function, and health-related quality of life.*

The fact that **physical health can improve our mental health** should not be understated. Numerous studies connect regular physical activity to enhanced emotional well-being.

Cancer and the treatments used can also cause disruption in the client's nutrition and body composition. Therefore, it is highly recommended to have nutritional guidance from a qualified healthcare professional to resolve any nutrient deficiencies, achieve or maintain a healthy weight, and preserve lean body mass.

The **American Cancer Society** lists the following Guidelines on Nutrition for Cancer prevention.

➢ *Limit processed meat and red meat*
➢ *Consume 2.5 cups of vegetables and fruits daily*
➢ *Choose whole grains instead of refined grain products*
➢ *If alcohol is consumed it should be limited to one drink per day for women and two drinks per day for men.*

Table 13-15 on page 632 of the Exercise Professional's Guide to Personal Training gives exercise guidelines for those with Cancer.

Osteoporosis is a condition associated with decreased ***bone mineral density (BMD)*** and deterioration in bone microarchitecture. About half of all Americans over 50 are expected to have osteoporosis. The statistics show that about 1 in 2 women, and 1 in 4 men over the age of 50 will break a bone due to osteoporosis. This condition causes structural weakness and increases the risk of a bone fracture. The most ***common fracture sites are the hip, spine, and wrist***. The incidence of hip fractures increases with age due to bone density decline, loss of muscular strength, and poor balance. ***90% of hip fractures occur from falls.***

Osteopenia is a condition in which bone mineral density (BMD) is lower than normal and is considered a precursor to osteoporosis.

Controllable factors that influence BMD include ***reproductive hormone levels, adequate levels of calcium and vitamin D, and physical activity***. The primary goal is to prevent the loss of bone mineral and to decrease the risk of falls and fractures. When working with clients that have osteoporosis, some activities may need to be modified or avoided to prevent further injury and falls. Clients with osteoporosis should obtain medical clearance from their physicians before beginning an exercise program.

Table 13-16 on page 637 of the Exercise Professional's Guide to Personal Training gives exercise guidelines for those with Osteoporosis.

Arthritis is a chronic degenerative condition of joints. ***Osteoarthritis*** is the most common form and the leading cause of disability in the U.S. ***Rheumatoid arthritis*** is an autoimmune disease characterized by *joint swelling, pain, and stiffness* that can lead to severe motion impairment.

Exercise programs for those with arthritis should be designed based on the functional status of the client. These programs should be designed in conjunction with the client's physician or physical therapist. The goals of the program are to improve cardiovascular fitness, increase muscular endurance and strength, and maintain or improve range of motion and flexibility around the affected joints.

Table 13-17 on page 641 of the Exercise Professional's Guide to Personal Training gives exercise guidelines for those with Arthritis.

Considerations for Clients with Obesity

Overweight and Obesity are the result of an energy imbalance between calories consumed and calories expended. Individuals with a Body Mass Index *(BMI) of 30 or above are considered obese.* In recent history, *energy intake* in the form of all types of food has increased and *energy expenditure* in the form of exercise or movement has decreased. As a whole, humans are eating more and moving less.

Even though this concept seems simple, it's much more nuanced for most people. Obesity is the result of a complex interaction between our *environment, genetic predisposition, and human behavior.* Everyone has different genetics, different preferences, different daily schedules, and stressors. These all have an impact on *what and when we eat*, and *how we feel afterward*. What works best for one person may not for another.

Environmental factors have increased our access to food and decreased our need to move frequently. Technology has also shifted our daily routines to where a lot of us are living and working in sedentary environments.

Genetics also play a role in the genetic predisposition to obesity. However, genes are not as important as lifestyle, which includes behavioral and environmental factors. Genetic predispositions to *obesity can be reduced by about 40% by being physically active.* Those who are genetically disposed to have a higher BMI benefit from regular exercise. However, genes do play a role in how people respond to diet and exercise. What works for one individual may not work as well for another.

Hormones can also play a role in body composition. Two key hormones related to energy metabolism regulation are *leptin* and *adiponectin.*

> **Leptin** helps regulate our food intake and energy expenditure. When fat cells decrease in size, leptin decreases as well which signals our brain to eat more. When fat cells increase in size so does leptin which signals us to eat less. With obesity, a decreased sensitivity to leptin occurs *(similar to insulin resistance in type 2 diabetes),* resulting in an inability to detect satiety *(feeling of fullness)* despite high energy stores and high levels of leptin. This creates a negative feedback loop and overconsumption.

> **Adiponectin** is involved in helping *insulin* regulate *glucose levels (blood sugar)* as well as *fatty acid breakdown (triglycerides).* If a person has a lot of body fat, then they will typically have lower levels of adiponectin. Low adiponectin combined with insulin resistance causes an increase in blood glucose levels which may lead to type 2 diabetes.

> **Immune Hormones** such as *cytokines* are also produced by fat tissue. Individuals with obesity tend to have an overreaction in terms of the releases of these inflammatory proteins. Both obesity and diabetes are associated with *chronic low-grade inflammation* which is a key risk factor in heart disease.

> **Appetite-regulating Hormones** are often referred to as the *gut hormones* because they are located in the gastrointestinal tract and signal hunger to trigger eating, and satiety to reduce appetite. **Ghrelin** is often called the *"hunger hormone"* which is secreted by the stomach and plays the chief role in appetite regulation.

Sleep and Stress

Sleep quality and quantity correlate with obesity as well. The reasons for this are complex and have been associated with *hunger, appetite, the immune system, stress, and inflammatory mediators.* Inadequate sleep also causes fatigue and reduced activity, compounding the problem. There are a lot of distractions and inputs in today's world. Technology has more people staying up later in front of screens *(working, browsing, or binge-watching shows.)* This keeps our bodies from downregulating properly to get in the quality sleep that is needed. The later we stay up hunger hormones also kick in, and we can end up overconsuming. It has been estimated that **58% of obstructive sleep apnea (OSA) is due to obesity.**

Obstructive Sleep Apnea (OSA) is a common disorder that causes pauses in breathing during sleep. This creates a vicious cycle of decreasing sleep, increasing weight, and worsening sleep apnea.

Stress is another big factor. The term *"stress"* has a negative connotation. It's commonly used to describe the negative effects that stress can have on us mentally and physically. This is actually describing the term **Distress**, which is a negative form of stress. **Anxiety, mental overwhelm, physical overtraining, lack of sleep, and poor eating habits** are all forms of distress. Our modern world is complex and filled with a lot of input and stressors. These contribute to many diseases and disorders, including obesity, and other eating-related disorders.

In today's society **food** *is one of the most* **overused** *tools to deal with stress and* **exercise** *is one of the most* **underused** *tools to deal with stress.*

Chronic stress that is not properly managed is what becomes problematic. Most **Acute stressors** are arguably beneficial, as long as we adapt to them.

- **Chronic** means reoccurring or long term.
- **Acute** refers to brief but intense.

It's helpful to **re-frame the way we think of stress**. Stress is simply our body's response to changes that create taxing demands. **Eustress** describes a positive form of stress that is beneficial for us. Exercise is one example that puts stress on our body and our response to that stimulus is to rebuild and become stronger. Hot and cold exposure are also forms of positive stress placed on the body in acute doses. Studies have shown that **regular sauna use is associated with a 40% decreased risk of all-cause mortality.** Heat shock proteins and other beneficial biological responses occur after being exposed to these stresses.

Stresses will always be around; it's **how we respond to them that makes all the difference.** We can help to **stack the conditions in our client's favor** by incorporating positive stresses and helping them mitigate the negative stressors. Regular exercise is one of the best ways to deal with mental stress, boost mood, reduce anxiety, and just feel better overall.

Weight Management

It is widely known that **3,500 calories = 1 pound of fat.** Theoretically creating a **500 calorie per day** deficit either by **restricting calories consumed, burning calories through exercise, or a combination of both** will result in a **loss of 1 pound per week.** However, this formula is based on a loss of fat tissue. Most people will also lose water weight and possibly lean tissue as well which has a lower energy content. In the early phases of energy restriction, weight loss is generally from water weight, while fat is mainly lost during the later phases. Combining exercise with caloric restriction helps to change the composition of the weight lost. Resistance training preserves the lean body tissue *(muscle)* which helps to burn more calories at rest **increasing Resting Metabolic Rate (RMR) / metabolism.**

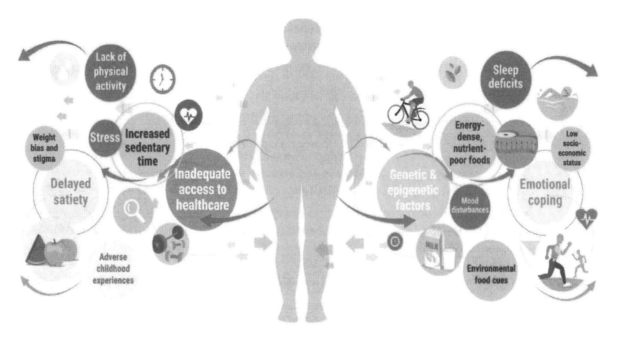

It's important to keep the basic concept in mind of **energy intake** vs **energy expenditure**, then implement a system and plan to find the right balance that works for your client's goals and lifestyle. A measured and practical approach is best that can be adhered to long-term. **Weight that is lost quickly is often regained quickly.** Restrictive diets and eating plans are also hard to maintain long-term. **Effective weight loss usually occurs at 1 – 2 pounds per week.** Make sure to stay within your scope of practice and only discuss general nutritional information and suggestions. Portion control, eating frequency, **consuming nutrient-dense foods** *(nuts, seeds, lean meats),* and **reducing energy-dense foods** *(simple carbs, sugary drinks)* with little nutritional value.

If calories are reduced to lose weight, it's important to maintain **adequate protein intake to build, repair, and maintain lean tissue.** Protein also helps to increase satiety *(feeling of fullness).*

The **NIH Body weight planner** is a useful tool for coming up with realistic goals for weight loss. **https://www.niddk.nih.gov/bwp**

ACE Mover Method and ABC Approach

Page 565 gives a great example of how to handle client's questions about diets using the ABC Approach. This approach is based on asking the right questions to allow the client to come to the answers on their own. You are there to help guide the thought process by asking open-ended questions and providing feedback as needed. Some good questions to ask about a diet plan include:

➢ *How does the diet cut calories?*

➢ *What is the nutrient density of the diet?*

➢ *Does the diet recommend exercise?*

➢ *Does it make sense?*

➢ *Where is the evidence?*

➢ *Does it meet your individual needs?*

➢ *How much does it cost?*

➢ *What kind of social support will it provide?*

➢ *How easy is it to adhere to the diet?*

Exercise Guidelines for Obesity

The goal is to increase energy expenditure aiming to expend more calories than are consumed to create an appropriate deficit for weight loss. Walking is a great way for overweight clients to get started since it requires no equipment, and is something humans already do on a regular basis. Emphasis should be placed on the ***total distance or time walked or ran for the week***; not necessarily how much is done per session. Walking for 20 minutes per day on 6 days of the week requires the same amount of energy as walking for 60 minutes 2 days per week. Even splitting up the exercise into smaller ***10 – 15-minute sessions adds up if done consistently***. A client can take a 15-minute walk on their lunch break and another 15-minute walk when they get home to total 30 minutes per day.

NEAT *(Non-Exercise Activity Thermogenesis)* relates to common activities of daily living that are related to lifestyle, but not specific exercise routines. This could involve redesigning the environments we live and work in to ***elicit more movement throughout the day.*** Getting a standing desk with a good footpad, or an ergonomic chair the encourages good posture and movement are some great options. Small but consistent actions will add to the overall energy expenditure and contribute to maintaining or losing weight.

Exercise selection should be based on the client's preferences and exercise history. ***We are more likely to repeat activities that we enjoy doing,*** so if a person has had success with a certain form of exercise in the past, it's beneficial to incorporate this into their current training program. Make sure to monitor any ***contraindications*** such as exercising in hot / humid environments, as overweight individuals have a harder time dissipating heat. Exercise should be altered as needed if the client has any joint-related or orthopedic issues. Recumbent bikes and elliptical trainers are great options for those who are overweight.

There is a **strong dose-response correlation** between the volume *(frequency, intensity, and duration)* of exercise and the total amount of fat loss. Studies done on *training durations of 12 - 18 weeks* showed that those who *exercised 150 minutes per week lost between 4.4 – 6.6 pounds* while those who *exercised for 225 – 420 minutes per week lost between 11 – 16.5 pounds.* This was without caloric restriction. However, the combination of exercise and sensible eating habits produce the best outcomes for long-term weight loss. The goal is to lose the weight and then maintain the new healthy body weight over the lifespan.

Remind your clients that **fitness-related improvements** are equally, if not more important than the loss of scale weight alone. Maintaining current body weight could be viewed as a win because they have stopped the cycle of gaining weight, and are now working towards going the other direction. Help them focus on the controllable factors of **increased physical activity and healthy eating** over the long term and the rest takes care of itself.

Cardiorespiratory Training should follow the same protocols as the general population using the **FITT principle.**

> - *Frequency* – Work up to at least 5 days per week of activity. Totaling 150 to 250 minutes each week to prevent significant weight gain, reduce associated chronic disease risk factors, and produce modest weight loss for individuals with overweight and obesity.
> - *Intensity* – Use the talk-test and RPE to determine exercise below VT1 for base training. This usually correlates to a moderate intensity or *"somewhat hard"* on the RPE scale 3 – 4 on 0 – 10 modern scale and 12 – 13 on the 6 – 20 classic scale.
> - *Time* – Exercise 30 – 60 minutes per day. Either in one session or broken up into smaller segments throughout the day.
> - *Type* – Perform low-impact, rhythmic exercise using large muscle groups.

Muscular Training helps to improve overall fitness and body composition. Muscle is denser than fat and takes up less space. It can alter appearance by creating a shift in the ratio of fat mass to lean mass. Even without a reduction in scale weight, people report looking better and feeling more comfortable in their clothing from muscular training adaptations, and subsequent increases in lean body mass. FITT recommendations for Muscular Training:

> - *Frequency* – Perform 2 – 3 days per week with a day of rest between sessions.
> - *Intensity* – Exercise at a moderate level 60 – 70% of 1RM for 8 – 12 reps for 2 – 4 sets. The focus should be on improving strength so that daily activities will be less challenging.
> - *Time* – A full-body muscular training session should take 20 – 30 minutes to complete. The exact time depends on the number of exercises and sets included.
> - *Type* – Train all of the major muscle groups using free weights and/or machines. Seated machine-based exercises are helpful in building strength in those who have biomechanical considerations such as mobility or balance issues. The form of resistance used is not as important as technique and largely depends on preference, training experience, and the client's goals.

Exercise Considerations Across the Lifespan

Youth: Physical inactivity, poor dietary habits, and other unhealthy behaviors established at a young age have a high probability of persisting into adulthood. This increases the risk of premature death. Children and adolescents from ages 6 – 17 years old should participate in *at least 60 minutes per day of moderate to vigorous-intensity exercise.* Children should also engage in muscle and bone-strengthening activities *at least three days per week.*

Physical literacy is a term used to describe the *ability, confidence, and desire* to be physically active for life. One of the best ways to get children physically active is to make it fun and engaging while prioritizing their effort, not necessarily their performance. Effort is a controllable factor and performance will increase as a result of consistent deliberate practice.

Children learn much more about behavior by *observing,* not necessarily listening to the words you say. Kids inherently know the true measure of a person is from their *actions, not words.* This explains why *inactive parents are nearly six times more likely to have inactive children.* Parents who give *consistent feedback by matching their actions with their words* set a great example for their children.

Examples of Physical Activities for the Youth can be found in Table 14-1 on page 656 of the Exercise Professional's Guide to Personal Training.

Table 14-2 on page 659 shows the FITT recommendations for Children and Adolescents.

Exercise for Women during Pregnancy and the Postpartum Period

Doctors used to encourage pregnant women to avoid exercise during pregnancy due to concerns of activity harming the baby. However, the *World Health Organization* and the *American College of Sports Medicine* have issued evidence-based recommendations indicating the benefits of exercise far outweigh the risks. In the absence of complications or contraindications, exercise during and after pregnancy is safe and desirable. It is important to request medical clearance from the client's physician if they also have *severe obesity, gestational diabetes, or hypertension.* Some chronic conditions may worsen during pregnancy such as *anemia, hypertension, seizure disorder, or hyperthyroidism,* and can be contraindications to activity during pregnancy. There is a PARmed-X evaluation form for pregnancy that can be found at **csep.ca**

During a healthy pregnancy, it is recommended that women gain 25 – 35 pounds. As the baby grows, a women's center of gravity moves upward and forward. This change in weight and COG may result in low back discomfort and affect balance and coordination. A focus early in the pregnancy on increasing posterior leg and trunk strength can help ready the body for the increased demand. Hormone levels also change, which can cause fatigue and nausea, especially in the first trimester. An increase in the hormone *relaxin* increases joint laxity and range of motion to prepare for birth. Since this affects all joints in the body, incorporating some stability training will help mitigate the joint instability caused by relaxin.

Performing exercises in a **prone** *(laying on stomach)* or **supine** *(laying on back)* position is **contraindicated** and not advised as a woman progresses into the advanced stages of pregnancy *(after 12 weeks / 2nd and 3rd Trimester).* This could cause decreased venous return and low blood pressure. Uncontrolled twisting motions of the torso are also contraindicated.

Make sure you are aware of the warning signs listed on **page 661 of the Exercise Professional's Guide** to discontinue exercise and refer to a medical professional if warranted.

Table 14-3 on page 663 of the Exercise Professional's Guide to Personal Training gives FITT recommendations for pregnant women.

A case study on exercise consistency throughout pregnancy using the ACE Mover Method and ABC Approach can be found on **page 664 of the Exercise Professional's Guide.**

Postpartum Guidelines

Exercise intensity should be increased gradually postnatal. It takes a few months post-pregnancy for women's bodies to adjust back to their pre-pregnant state. Especially the core and pelvic floor muscles. Stabilization and core exercises are beneficial to help strengthen the core and improve functional capacity.

Diastasis Recti is the separation of the two muscle bellies of the rectus abdominis. This is a common condition in women who are pregnant.

Figures 14-1 thru 14-5 on pages 668 – 669 of the Exercise Professional's Guide show common exercises to incorporate that may reduce the risk of diastasis recti and support the low back and pelvic floor. These included *quadruped transverse abdominis isometric contractions, wide stance squat with a dumbbell, bridges with a yoga block or ball between legs, bent knee alternating heel taps, and bird dogs.*

Exercise for Older Adults

Muscle mass, bone mass, balance, and coordination all tend to decline with age. The decreased effectiveness of the neuromuscular system can cause balance issues, and a greater risk for falls in the older population. Physical activity that includes strength training can help maintain and improve muscle mass and bone mineral density. Balancing training can improve reactivity and coordination. All of which reduce the risk of injury and improve the overall quality of life. The incidence of chronic diseases and arthritis also drastically increase with older age. A thorough preparticipation health screening must be conducted by the personal trainer.

Physical activity has been shown to improve cognitive function in older individuals. Improved cognitive ability, along with the important human connection and socialization associated with exercising helps with both mental health and mental capacity.

***Table 14-4 on page 673 of the Exercise Professional's Guide gives FITT recommendations for older adults.**

Domain IV: Professional Conduct, Safety, & Risk Management

Fulfill professional responsibilities through continuing education, collaboration with allied health professionals, and adherence to industry standards and practices necessary to protect clients, facility operators, and the personal trainer.

ACE Certified Personal Trainer Scope of Practice

Read and understand the ACE Certified Personal Trainers' scope of practice. ***See Table 1-2 on page 12 and Figure 1-2 on page 13 of the Exercise Professional's Guide to Personal Training.***

Claims related to violations of the scope of practice most frequently occur in the area of supplements. Unless a personal trainer is also a registered dietitian or a physician, he or she does not have the expertise or legal qualifications necessary to recommend supplements.

An ACE Certified Personal Trainer (CPT) must ***always*** operate within their ***scope of practice*** and refer clients to other ***allied healthcare professionals*** when necessary. Especially when providing a personal opinion that could be taken as professional advice. It's helpful to network with physicians, physical therapists, registered dietitians, and other healthcare specialists.

Referrals can take place at any point during the client-trainer relationship.
(During the initial screening, a training session or evaluations down the line)

Read and understand the **ACE Code of Ethics** in the ***Appendix from pages 785 – 790 of the Exercise Professional's Guide to Personal Training.***

Certification Period and Renewal

ACE Certifications are valid for **2 years and require 20 hours of ACE-approved continuing education (2.0 CECs)** to maintain certification. Trainers must also maintain current ***cardiopulmonary resuscitation (CPR)*** and ***automated external defibrillator (AED)*** certifications.

Business Plan

Personal trainers must make the important decision to either work for an employer, work as an independent contractor, or start their own training business as an entrepreneur. Working for an employer is a good option for personal trainers who are just starting out as they can learn about the industry without having to take the time and financial risks involved with operating a business on their own. Once they gain experience, they can venture off as an independent contractor or start their own business.

Personal trainers should take some time conducting market research to ensure the target demographic *(prospective customers)* have the means and access to the trainer's potential work environments. Developing a unique skillset that is tailored to the specific goals of this customer base will help the trainer build their *"brand"* of training.

A business plan should cover all of the following: ***Executive summary, Business description, Marketing plan, Operational plan, Risk analysis, Decision-making criteria.***

A **Financial plan** should provide specific details for how a business will generate cash flow and produce a profit. The personal trainer should be as specific as possible and consider all of the potential issues related to cash flow in the planning process. This will allow them to focus time on the operation once the business is open.

Personal trainers should stay up to date on the standards of care and accepted business practices. Regular consultation with an attorney who is aware of the unique laws governing the trainer's city, state, and county will help to ensure that legal responsibilities are met and upheld. This will help to mitigate potential litigation and other legal concerns.

The following are the most popular times for clients to work with trainers:

- Morning 5AM – 9AM *(before work)*
- Afternoon 12PM – 2PM *(lunch break)*
- Evening 4PM – 8PM *(after work)*

Six Basic Business Models

Sole Proprietorship: One person owns the business. This has benefits because you have full control over business decisions but it also means that you literally are your business. A common term used is *"bottleneck"* If you take a vacation or get sick there is no one available to keep the business running in your absence. This business structure also puts you at full responsibility for legal issues. A lawsuit filed against a sole proprietor can go after both business and personal finances such as your home or vehicles.

Partnership: Two or more people who form a business together. Any potential partnership can become contentious and should not be entered without considerable contemplation and legal advice.

Corporation: A formal business entity subject to laws, regulations, and the demands of stockholders. A corporation is a legal entity completely separate from its owners and managers.

S-Corporation (Subchapter Corporation): Combines the advantages of sole proprietorship, partnership, and corporation business models. They are shielded from personal liability. A suitable alternative for small businesses.

Limited Liability Company (LLC): Flexible for small and medium-sized businesses and generally have more advantages than partnerships or S corporations.

Independent Contractor: Provides certain services for other individuals or businesses. There is a difference between an *independent contractor* who is paid per job or task on a short-term basis and an *employee* who works for an employer and is compensated on a regular basis.

Advantages and Disadvantages of these various business structures can be found in Table 16-1 on page 745 of the Exercise Professional's Guide to Personal Training.

Legal Documentation and Laws

Contracts provide the best method to ensure that all aspects of a relationship are properly established. Whether a trainer works as an independent contractor or employee the basic tenets of contract law should be understood. The following elements are necessary to create a binding contract:

- An offer and acceptance with a mutual agreement of terms
- Consideration *(an exchange of valuable items, such as money for services)*
- Legality *(acceptable under the law)*
- Ability of the parties to enter into a contract concerning legal age and mental capacity

Negligence: A failure to perform as a reasonable and prudent professional would perform under similar circumstances. A reasonable and prudent person is someone who adheres to the established standard of care. Slip-and-fall injuries, equipment issues, free weights, weight machines, cardiovascular machines, and claims of sexual harassment are common areas of negligence seen in training settings. Negligence can be an *act of omission* if a trainer fails to act or an *act of commission* if the trainer acts inappropriately. This could include failing to spot a client during an exercise or having them perform a contraindicated exercise if they have a known issue. A plaintiff must prove the following four elements in a negligence claim.

- *Duty* – the defendant *(trainer)* had a duty to protect the plaintiff *(client)* from injury.
- *Breach of duty* – The trainer failed to uphold the standard of care necessary.
- *Damages* or injury to the plaintiff *(client)* occurred.
- *Proximate cause* – Damage or injury to the plaintiff was caused by the defendant's breach of duty.

Comparative negligence is when more than one person is at fault for an incident or injury.

Stay up to date on the standards of care and accepted business practices. Regular consultation with an attorney who is aware of the unique laws governing the trainer's city, state, and county will help to ensure that legal responsibilities are met and upheld. This will help to mitigate potential litigation and other legal concerns. Forms such as an *Agreement to participate, Informed consent, and Waivers* are ways that trainers can make clients aware of inherent risks involved in participation and avoid or defend against potential negligence claims.

Agreement to participate is a signed document that indicates the client is aware of the inherent risks and potential injuries that can occur from participation in exercise. A sample agreement to participate form can be found in *Figure 16-1 on page 753 of the Exercise Professional's Guide.*

Informed consent is a written statement signed by a client prior to testing that informs them of testing purposes, process, and all potential risks and discomforts. A sample informed consent form can be found in *Figure 16-2 on page 754 of the Exercise Professional's Guide.*

Waiver: Voluntary abandonment of a right to file suit; but is not always legally binding. Investigation with an attorney before creating a waiver is recommended as each state has its own rules regarding waivers. It is recommended that personal trainers utilize their own waivers in addition to any waivers potentially signed by a client when they joined the fitness center or club where the trainer is employed. A sample waiver form can be found in *Figure 16-3 on page 757 Exercise Professional's Guide.*

Waivers typically do not protect trainers from injuries directly caused by *gross negligence*, which is an action that demonstrates recklessness or a willful disregard for the safety of others.

The rise in *virtual personal training* online has made it easier than ever for trainers to connect with their clients. However, personal trainers should consult with an attorney prior to implementing any online sessions. Negligence laws and personal trainer responsibility may be different in various jurisdictions and there could be special stipulations regarding online training.

The goal is to have a safe exercise environment where mistakes are mitigated, injuries limited, and potential lawsuits completely avoided. Legal standards require that clients be given *"adequate and proper"* instruction before and during activity. Personal trainers should avoid touching clients unless it is essential for proper instruction and always obtain permission.

Accurately written record-keeping of a client's *medical history, exercise record, incident reports, and any correspondence* is essential for trainers. From the perspective of the court system, if information is not written down, then it did not occur and does not exist. Keeping records current and adding new information is also a great way to track the progress of your client from the baseline they started at.

HIPAA *(Health Insurance Portability and Accountability Act)*: Law that requires health care professionals to have strict policies regarding the safety and security of private records. Written permission from the client must be obtained before sharing confidential information with an outside party such as another allied healthcare professional. This also includes posting a client's results *(before* and *after photos, for marketing purposes, or on social media).* A sample HIPAA permission form can be found in *Figure 16-4 on page 763 Exercise Professional's Guide.*

SOAP Notes *(Subjective, Objective, Assessment, and Plan)* can be used to document client progress.

- **Subjective information**: Client observations including their own status report, a description of symptoms, challenges with the program, and progress made.
- **Objective**: Measurements taken such as heart rate, blood pressure, height, weight, age, posture, assessment results, as well as exercise and nutrition log information.
- **Assessment**: A summary of the client's current status based on subjective and objective observations and measurements.
- **Plan**: A description of the next steps in the program based on the assessment.

Risk Management Program

Risk management is a process whereby a service or program is delivered in a manner to fully conform to the most relevant standards of practice, and that uses operational strategies to ensure day-to-day fulfillment, ensure optimum achievement of desired client outcomes, and minimize the risk of harm to clients. Risk management protocols should consist of the following five steps:

➢ **Risk identification** involves the specification of all risks that may be encountered in the areas of instruction, supervision, facilities, equipment, contracts, and business structure.

➢ **Risk evaluation** is when the personal trainer reviews each risk, with consideration given to the probability that the risk could occur and, if so, what would be the conceivable severity

➢ **Selection of an approach for managing each risk** which include the following methods.
  - *Avoidance* by removing the possibility of danger and injury by eliminating the activity.
  - *Transfer* by moving the risk to others through waivers and insurance policies.
  - *Reduction* by modifying the activity to reduce the risks.
  - *Retention* of risk in the low category where the benefits far outweigh the potential risks. A certain amount of risk is inherent to most activities including exercising and driving a car.

➢ **Implementation** is instituting the plan.

➢ **Evaluation** involves continually assessing the outcome of risk-management endeavors.

The following forms should be kept and maintained to ensure business practices conform to the standards set by professional organizations:

1) **Preactivity Screening Form (PAR-Q)**
2) **Health History Questionnaire**
3) **Physician's Statement and Medical Clearance Form**
4) **Fitness Assessment or Evaluation Form**
5) **Release, Waiver, or Informed Consent**
6) **Client Progress Notes**
7) **Incident Reports**

A business and/or personal trainer should carry *professional liability insurance* which transfers the risk to the insurance company in the event of an incident or claim by a client. The best insurance policies cover the cost of legal defense and any claims awarded. ACE recommends retaining at least 1 million in coverage. The following is a link for reputable insurance carriers who specialize in the fitness industry ➔ www.ACEfitness.org/insurancecenter/

Emergency Procedures

All organizations or personal trainers that operate independently must have an emergency action plan in place. When an incident occurs, the personal trainer should first ensure the safety of all individuals involved and then activate EMS if warranted. Once the immediate safety concern has passed, the personal trainer should complete an incident report detailing facts related to the incident. The facility should also have an AED onsite. Personal trainers and staff who are responsible for working directly with clients must have current **CPR (Cardiopulmonary Resuscitation)** and **AED (Automated External Defibrillator)** certifications. Failure to abide by the emergency procedures can expose the trainer to legal liability.

Injury Prevention Program

An area of Tort Law called ***"premises liability"*** regulates any incidents that result from conditions of the physical setting where training activities occur. Any training setting or premises must have a reasonably safe environment. Exercise equipment service plans along with routine inspections and maintenance of equipment should be performed to reduce the potential risk of injury. If an unsafe condition is noticed, the trainer should notify the facility's management and avoid that area until it has been addressed. Providing a safe environment along with the emergency action plan mentioned above will help to mitigate potential liability for incidents that may occur during a training session. ****The number one claim against fitness facilities and professionals is for injuries related to falls on the training premises.***

When to call 9-1-1

It is appropriate to call emergency medical services (EMS) when there is a life-threatening situation or anything that requires immediate medical attention. The following situations where someone is seriously ill, is not breathing, has an open wound to the chest, or is bleeding profusely warrant contacting 9-1-1.

Cardiac arrest is the cessation of heart function when a person loses consciousness, has no pulse, and stops breathing. The following *Chain of Survival (four steps)* developed by the *American Heart Association (AHA)* can increase the likelihood of survival:

> ➢ Early access
> ➢ Early CPR
> ➢ Early defibrillation
> ➢ Early advanced care

Without treatment, the person's chance of survival decreases by 10% for every minute that passes. CPR should ideally begin within two minutes of the onset of cardiac arrest. EMS usually takes an average of 7-10 minutes to arrive once contacted so CPR should be performed by a bystander, friend, family member, or stranger as it can more than double the chance of survival.

Common Medical Emergencies and Injuries

Dyspnea occurs when a person has difficult and labored breathing. In some situations, dyspnea can come on suddenly and be very uncomfortable and even life-threatening. Trainers should be aware of the signs of respiratory distress including poor movement of the chest wall, flaring of the nostrils, straining of the neck muscles, poor air exchange from the mouth and nose, pale sweaty skin, and **Cyanosis** *(a bluish color that develops around the lips, nose, fingernails, and inner lining of the eyes)*. To assess breathing in an unconscious person, a personal trainer should feel for airflow on their own cheek while looking for the chest to rise and fall while also listening for unusual snoring, gurgling, or high-pitched sounds that may indicate a partial airway blockage. If the person is **apneic** *(not breathing)* no chest movement or sounds indicating air movement, the personal trainer should give breaths. If there is no pulse then CPR should be initiated.

Choking: A person who is choking will have a partially or entirely blocked airway. If the person cannot breathe, make sounds, or has a very quiet cough, or if a child cannot cry, the blockage is severe. The **Heimlich maneuver** should be performed. The rescuer should stand behind the victim with both arms wrapped around the victim's waist, make a fist with one hand, and put the thumb side just above the victim's belly button. The other hand should grab this fist and perform several upward thrusts to compress the diaphragm and force the object out of the victim's airway. If the victim is very large or in the late stages of pregnancy, the rescuer can wrap their arms around the victim's breastbone instead of the abdomen. If the Heimlich maneuver does not work, the victim may become unconscious. If this occurs someone should call for help and CPR should be initiated.

Heart Attack: A heart attack is caused by an obstruction in a coronary vessel that prevents part of the heart muscle from getting adequate blood flow and oxygen. The warning signs and symptoms of a heart attack include ***angina pectoris*** *(chest pain / pressure)*, pain can also be felt in one or both arms *(usually the left arm)*, the neck, jaw, shoulder, or stomach, there can also be shortness of breath, nausea, a cold sweat, and lightheadedness. Most heart attack warning signs have a gradual onset that is not sudden and intense. Delay in treatment can be fatal. Personal trainers should be able to recognize signs of a heart attack as the person experiencing the symptoms may not realize what is happening or be in denial.

Contraindicated exercises: Movements or positions that are not recommended due to the potential injury risk associated. Examples include *straight-leg sit-ups, double leg raises, standing bent over toe touch, cervical, and lumbar hyperextension.*

Exercising in the Heat

Dissipating internal body heat is more difficult when exercising in the heat, especially in hot and humid environments where sweat does not evaporate readily to cool the body. Various types of heat stress can occur with exercise in hot and humid conditions such as heat edema, heat cramps, or more serious conditions such as heat exhaustion, and heat stroke. Signs and symptoms of heat exhaustion and heat stroke are listed below along with appropriate responses to each.

	Signs and Symptoms	*Appropriate Response*
Heat Exhaustion	Weak, rapid pulse Low blood pressure Headache Nausea Dizziness General weakness Paleness Profuse sweating ***Cold, clammy skin**	Stop exercising Move to a cool, ventilated area Lie down and elevate feet 12 – 18 inches (30 – 46 cm) Give fluids Monitor temperature
Heat Stroke	***Hot, dry skin** Bright red skin color Rapid, strong pulse Labored breathing Elevated body core temperature (>104° F or 40° C)	Stop exercising Remove as much clothing as feasible Try to cool the body immediately in any way possible (wet towels, ice packs/baths, fan alcohol rubs) Give fluids Transport to the emergency room immediately.

Figure 8-12 on page 271 of the Exercise Professional's Guide to Personal Training shows a heat index chart based on relative humidity and temperature. It gives heat stress risk with physical activity based on increased temperatures. Clients should avoid exercise in extremely hot and humid conditions with a wet bulb global temperature (WBGT) above 82°F.

Tips for exercising in the Heat

- Begin gradually *(acclimation takes 9 – 14 days)*

- Always wear lightweight, well-ventilated clothing

- Never wear impermeable or nonbreathable garments

- Replace body fluids as they are lost *(don't rely on thirst alone, drink at regular intervals, weigh yourself pre* and *post-workout if possible, to estimate fluid loss)* See the Fluid Recommendations in *Table 8-3 on page 272 of the Exercise Professional's Guide.*

Exercising in the Cold

Hypothermia and frostbite can occur when exposed to extremely cold climates or conditions. Proper preparation is necessary to avoid overexposure to the cold. Clothing should be layered to trap body heat and help maintain body temperature. Hats and gloves can also be used to prevent frostbite in exposed areas. There are 3 primary ways the body avoids excessive heat loss: *peripheral vasoconstriction, non-shivering thermogenesis, and shivering.* Shivering kicks in if the first two are insufficient to maintain internal temperature. Involuntary shivering of the skeletal muscles can increase the body's *rate of heat production 4 – 5 times.*

Figure 8-13 on page 273 of the Exercise Professional's Guide to Personal Training gives windchill factors for exercising in the cold. It should also be noted that *the body loses heat four times faster in water than it does in air of the same temperature.*

Tips for exercising in the Cold

- Wear several layers of clothing *(remove / replace as needed)*

- Allow for adequate ventilation of sweat

- Wear breathable clothing *(give off heat during exercise and retain during rest periods)* Wet sweaty clothes will extract more heat from the body.)

- Replace body fluids in the cold, just as in the heat.

- Monitor body weight.

Exercising at Higher Altitudes and Air Pollution

A person exercising at a high altitude will not be able to deliver as much oxygen to the exercising muscles so exercise intensity should be reduced. The first phase of acclimatization takes place in approximately two weeks. However, it could take several months to fully acclimate to a higher altitude.

Signs and symptoms of *altitude sickness* include *shortness of breath, headache, lightheadedness, and nausea.* These can generally be avoided by starting slow and allowing the body to acclimatize before increasing exercise intensity.

Musculoskeletal Injuries

Throughout your training career, you may encounter clients with a pre-existing injury or a current client who shows up with a new injury. It's important to recognize the difference between **pain from an injury** or **discomfort from exercise.** Creating a training program that addresses any musculoskeletal issues associated with the injury is an important part of recovery.

Stay within your **scope of practice** and work closely with the client's physical therapist, or physician using their activity recommendations and clearance. Trainers do not **evaluate, assess, or diagnose injuries, illness, muscle, or joint pain.**

The initial screening process should make trainers aware of clients who are at an increased risk of injury due to age, previous injury history, deconditioned musculature, and/or disease. A thoughtful program design and use of periodization are essential to prevent injuries from occurring.

Decreases in **Flexibility and Elasticity** could be the cause or consequence of injury.

Assessing Clients with Musculoskeletal Conditions

> Explain that the assessment is going to help determine a starting point for safe exercise programming. Look out for wincing, hesitation, slowed or erratic pace, and loss of balance. These can indicate pain or neurological inhibition *"like a kink in a garden hose"* limiting movement.

> Tell the client that they may request a modification for any movement.

> Explain the perceived pain scale 0 – 10 shown in *Figure 15-4 on page 691 of the Exercise Professional's Guide to Personal Training* and ask if they are in pain.

> Inform the client that they should only move within a pain-free ROM.

> Ask the client if they have any questions or concerns

A case study of addressing a client's concerns about pain can be found on page 692 of the Exercise Professional's Guide utilizing the ACE Mover Method and ABC Approach.

Programming Considerations for Clients with Musculoskeletal Issues

Pain is a physical event marked by neural firing, but pain itself is a subjective sensation.

Perceived pain is generally measured on a scale of 0 – 10 with *0 being no pain / 5 being moderate pain / and 10 being the worst pain possible.* When clients indicate that pain is above a 3 then exercise should stop and modification to that exercise or a different exercise should be chosen. Encourage the client to communicate any amount of pain during exercise so that it can be regulated accordingly.

When *physical pain is chronic* it can have a *psychological impact* on the individual experiencing the pain affecting their mental health. Feelings of anger, hopelessness, and sadness can manifest as depression and anxiety. Exercise and staying active as tolerated is a great way to cope with chronic pain. Acknowledging your client's feelings about exercise and during exercise helps to build rapport and increase their likelihood of exercise adherence.

A case study for helping a client with pain reframe exercise intensity can be found on page 699 of the Exercise Professional's Guide utilizing the ACE Mover Method and ABC Approach.

Common Overuse Conditions

Overuse conditions occur when tissues cannot withstand the forces put upon them over time. These are typically caused by repetitive movements or faulty body mechanics.

Tendinitis, Bursitis, and Fasciitis *"itis"* means *"inflammation"*

- **Tendinitis** is inflammation of a tendon.
- **Bursitis** is the inflammation of the bursa sac. These usually occur from repetitive stress and overuse.
- **Fasciitis** is the inflammation of the connective tissue called fascia. Plantar fasciitis of the foot and IT Band syndrome are two common conditions.

Stress Fractures occur when repetitive stress is placed on a bone that is not strong enough to withstand these forces. This is caused by an imbalance in *bone formation* and *bone resorption.* **Bone resorption** is when bones break down to release minerals such as calcium from bone tissue to the blood. The tibia bone in the lower leg is a common spot for stress fractures. Stress fractures are different from shin splints and will have a single point of tenderness and worsen with weight-bearing activity. If a client shows any symptoms of a stress fracture they should be referred to a physician for diagnosis and treatment.

Acute and Chronic Injuries

- ➢ **Acute injuries** are quick and can be pinpointed such as rolling an ankle or pulling a muscle.
- ➢ **Chronic injuries** are those that may begin gradually such as low back pain but persist for more than six months.

Common Acute Injuries

Muscle Strains are injuries in which a muscle works beyond its capacity, resulting in tears in the muscle fibers. Strains are categorized by severity using a grading system.

- ➤ **Grade I** strains are *mild*. Though tender or painful, the strength of the muscle remains normal.

- ➤ **Grade II** strains are *moderate*. These include more severe pain and swelling that will likely cause weakness and decreased range of motion.

- ➤ **Grade III** strains are *severe* and indicate a complete tear of the muscle. The client may feel a sudden *"tear"* or *"pop"* accompanied by immediate pain and loss of function. Pain, swelling, and discoloration may also be present.

Ligament Sprains are usually caused by external forces of contact. This force is referred to as the *mechanism of injury*. They can also be non-contact when an individual is unable to maintain joint stability during movement and stretches a ligament to the point of injury. This is referred to as *ground reaction force.*

- ➤ **Grade I** sprains are *minimal*. There is minimal tenderness and swelling.

- ➤ **Grade II** sprains are *moderate*. These include more tenderness and swelling that will likely cause a decreased range of motion and possible instability.

- ➤ **Grade III** sprains are *severe* and indicate a complete tear of the ligament. There is significant tenderness, swelling, and instability.

Healing time of strains and sprains depends on the severity. Grade I injuries usually feel better within several days to a few weeks. Whereas a Grade III injury will take much longer and may require surgical intervention in order to regain full strength and function.

Cartilage provides shock absorption, stability, joint congruency, lubrication, and proprioception. It is found between bony structures of the joints. The knee is a common site for cartilage damage due to compression and shearing forces. The knee is considered a stable joint as it mostly hinges with minimal lateral movement. However, it is between two very mobile joints of the ankle and hip. This is also why ACL knee injuries are so common in sports. *See the kinetic chain diagram on page 357 of the Exercise Professional's Guide to Personal Training.*

Bone Fractures occur from impact or stress to the bone. They are less common in the personal training environment but it is important to recognize that conditions like osteoporosis can increase the likelihood. The trainer should be aware and ready to activate EMS if a fracture occurs.

Head, Neck, and Back Injuries

A **concussion** is a brain injury that causes a change in mental state. Concussions commonly occur in contact sports, car accidents, or as the result of falls or blows to the head. Concussions may or may not cause loss of consciousness. The brain is particularly vulnerable following a concussion so individuals who have experienced a concussion must be removed immediately from activity. They should be kept from activity until clearance has been given by a qualified healthcare professional. A concussion causes a variety of physical, cognitive, and emotional symptoms, which may not be recognized as the initial signs can be subtle. The first signs are often confusion and disorientation. Personal trainers should be aware of the following warning signs following a possible brain injury:

- Amnesia
- Confusion
- Memory loss
- Headache
- Drowsiness
- Loss of consciousness
- Impaired speech
- Tinnitus
- Unequal pupil size
- Nausea
- Vomiting
- Balance problems or dizziness
- Blurry or double vision
- Sensitivity to light or noise
- Any change in the individual's behavior, thinking, or physical function

*Note: There are common misconceptions between loss of consciousness and concussions. A loss of consciousness does not always accompany a concussion, and if a person does not lose consciousness it does not mean the concussion is minor. Trainers must understand that no concussion (brain injury) is ever minor.

Neck and Back injuries are often muscle strains that may have happened during exercise. They should be treated like any other strain and rested to allow healing.

Disc injuries are also possible from compression and shearing forces applied to the spine. Discs are made of collagen and act as a cushion between our vertebrae. *Figure 15-3 on page 688 of the Exercise Professional's Guide to Personal Training shows the anatomy of a vertebral disc.* Disc injuries can cause bulging or herniation of the disc which can press on the nerves causing pain and nerve spasms. If a disc injury is suspected, immediate referral to a doctor is needed.

If a person with back pain is experiencing nerve symptoms down their hips and legs then a disc issue is suspected. Although trainers do not diagnose or treat injuries it's helpful to be aware of the symptoms to warrant a referral. There are charts online that show the nerve roots and areas they control → *https://www.healthline.com/health/dermatome*

Common Conditions of the Spine

A physically inactive lifestyle, coupled with increased time spent sitting makes a person particularly vulnerable to muscle stiffness or injury along the spine. Even those who exercise on a regular basis are still likely to have muscular imbalances if the majority of their day is spent sedentary. *"Our bodies take the shape of the positions we are in the majority of the time."* This is a good mental anchor to keep in mind. Thoughtful program design that is consistently followed can improve mobility, postural alignment, and strength of the muscles along the spine.

Neck - Forward head position is a common posture alignment issue that places increased stress on the muscles of the neck. *Figure 15-14 on page 707 of the Exercise Professional's Guide to Personal Training* shows the *ideal alignment of the head and spine.* Good indicators are if the *cheekbone aligns with the clavicle (collarbone)* and the *ear aligning with the AC joint on top of the shoulder.*

The following steps can be followed to help improve neck function.

- *First,* observe the posture of the entire spine. Especially the relationship between the neck position and thoracic spine and shoulder. Forward head often occurs in conjunction with rounded shoulders and the kyphosis deviation. Address the spine and shoulder position first if faulty posture is observed.

- *Next,* introduce gentle movement and stretching that can be executed by the client at any time of the day when discomfort occurs.

- *Finally,* refer to a physician if the pain is severe or persistent.

Low Back pain most often occurs in individuals between 30 and 50 years of age. It is estimated that *80% of adults will experience acute low back pain at some point and that 30% of cases become chronic.* Low back pain has a variety of causes. A common dysfunction associated with low back pain is *exaggerated lordosis.* Depending on the cause of the pain, correcting the posture may help decrease pain and reduce the stress placed on the low back. Tight erector spinae, hip flexors, and potential weakness in the glutes and posterior muscles can cause this deviation and the associated low back pain. Program design should involve static stretching of the tight overactive muscles along with exercises to improve the range of motion of the hips and strengthening of the gluteal muscles, hamstrings, rectus abdominis, and internal and external obliques. *A sample daily routine for Enhancing low-back health can be found on page 710 of the Exercise Professional's Guide to Personal Training.*

The following steps can be followed to address and improve low-back function.

- *First,* address any imbalance between the right and left sides.
- *Next,* address any anterior / posterior postural imbalance (lordosis / kyphosis)
- *Then,* increase functional internal and external rotation of the hip.
- *Finally,* strengthen the posterior chain, especially the hamstrings and gluteal muscles to provide support.

Common Conditions of the Upper Extremities

The Shoulder joint has the greatest range of motion of any joint in the body. This leaves it susceptible to injury from improper movement mechanics and/or muscular / joint imbalance.

Figure 15-5 on page 702 of the Exercise Professional's Guide to Personal Training shows a diagram of the rotator cuff muscles and their locations. They can be remembered by the acronym SITS.

Rotator Cuff: Supraspinatus, Infraspinatus, Teres minor, Subscapularis (**SITS**)

- *Supraspinatus*: Abducts the glenohumeral *(shoulder)* joint
- *Infraspinatus*: Externally rotates the glenohumeral *(shoulder)* joint
- *Teres minor*: Externally rotates the glenohumeral *(shoulder)* joint
- *Subscapularis*: Internally rotates the glenohumeral *(shoulder)* joint

Weak shoulder musculature along with forward head and rounded shoulders *(kyphosis)* can cause compression and subsequent inflammation of the shoulder joint. This can lead to *impingement syndrome.* Exercises to improve shoulder function should work on building strength of the stabilizing muscles and improving posture to open space for the shoulder to move through a full range of motion.

- *First,* address any postural imbalances that may cause impingement or decreased space between the acromion process and the humeral head.
- *Next,* strengthening the scapular stabilizing muscles including the rotator cuff muscles, lower traps, rhomboids, and serratus anterior.
- *Then,* improve the strength of the anterior shoulder muscles *(deltoids)* and pectoralis major through controlled pushing motion.
- *Finally,* you can begin to introduce overhead activities as tolerated to further improve function, strength, and stability of the shoulder.

Figures 15-8 thru 15-10 on pages 704 and 705 of the Exercise Professional's Guide to Personal Training give sample exercise progressions for the shoulder. Seated Rows, serratus punch, along with stabilization exercises like the bird dog and farmers carry are good options.

Scapular pull-ups can also be beneficial. This is where you grab a pull-up bar with an overhand *(pronated)* grip with thumbs out, then retract and depress the scapula while keeping the arms completely straight. It can be regressed by using a lower bar with feet on the ground or a resistance band to reduce the bodyweight load for clients who are not strong enough to hold the *dead hang position.*

Elbow, Wrist, and Hand

Tennis and Golfers elbow are common conditions of the elbow. ***Tennis elbow*** affects the tendon on the outside of the elbow which is attached to the muscles involved in ***wrist extension*** such as a backhand stroke in tennis. ***Golfer's elbow*** affects the tendon connection on the inside of the elbow that is attached to the ***wrist flexor muscles***. In either case, overuse is typically the cause of the inflammation.

Remember that tendons and connective tissue take longer to adapt than muscles. When strength gains outpace connective tissue adaptations then inflammation and issues can arise if appropriate program progression is not followed.

When tendons are inflamed the training protocol should avoid adding stress to this area by adjusting or modifying exercises involving wrist flexion, extension, and gripping.

Carpal tunnel syndrome is caused by inflammation of the flexor tendons that pass under the bottom of the wrist. This causes compression of the median nerve and subsequent pain and numbness. The same exercise protocol is recommended as with the golfer and tennis elbow. Adding in ***neutral grip exercises*** can also be beneficial. Such as doing push-ups on neutral grip handles instead of with hands on the floor.

The ACE Guide gives progressive steps that can be followed for improving elbow, wrist, and hand function.

- ***First,*** limit overuse, adjusting grip as necessary for pushing and pulling movements.

- ***Next,*** increase ROM through gentle stretches in all planes of motion.

- ***Then,*** improve the strength of the wrist and hand through exercises involving wrist flexion and extension using appropriate progressions.

- ***Finally,*** slowly introduce volume to pulling exercises, as tolerated.

Common Conditions of the Lower Extremities

HIP – Dysfunction at the hip may be caused by a lack of strength, stability, or mobility. The hip is a ball and socket joint like the shoulder but is more stable due to the deep bony socket that limits ROM. Dysfunction at the hip can cause pain up the kinetic chain into the lower back and down the chain into the knees.

Piriformis Syndrome is a condition where the piriformis muscle becomes tight, or inflamed, causing compression of the **sciatic nerve** that runs next to the piriformis. In as much as *22% of the population,* the sciatic nerve actually splits and runs through the piriformis muscle. These people more prone to this condition. *Figures 15-21 and 15-22 on page 714 of the Exercise Professional's Guide to Personal Training* show diagrams of the sciatic nerve and deep rotators of the hip including the piriformis.

Program design for those with piriformis syndrome should focus on balancing the position of the right and left pelvis by inhibiting the tight overactive muscles and strengthening the underactive muscles. Also incorporating *closed chain internal and external hip rotation* exercises to improve mobility and stability of the hip. Exercises such as the *lift-and-chop* or a *shin box flow* in the 90/90 position on the ground are some good options.

Arthritis and hip replacements are also common conditions with the older population. It is essential to progress slowly for those with these conditions increasing intensities as tolerated and modifying exercises when warranted.

The following steps can be followed to address and improve hip function.

- *First,* address any imbalance between the right and left sides.
- *Next,* improve ROM of hip internal and external rotation, as well as single-leg stance stability.
- *Then,* improve hip-hinge mobility and stability.
- *Lastly,* improve the strength of the muscles of the posterior chain.

KNEE – Common conditions of the knee include *IT band friction syndrome, tendinitis, patellofemoral pain syndrome, and chondromalacia.*

Figures 15-23 thru 15-31 on pages 716 – 720 of the Exercise Professional's Guide to Personal Training show diagrams and descriptions of these conditions. The following steps can be followed to address and improve knee function.

- *First,* address any imbalance between the right and left sides. If muscles are tight on one side they should be stretched while the opposing side should be strengthened.

- *Next,* address any tightness and instability in the hip, ankle, and foot that may be contributing to femoral internal rotation *(knee valgus)* Generally self-myofascial release and stretching to inhibit the tight surrounding musculature is the first step to alleviating these common conditions.

- *Then,* improve hip-hinge mobility and stability.

- *Lastly,* improve the strength of the muscles of the posterior chain

Squatting is a required movement for most *activities of daily living ADL*. Lack of coordination during hip hinging and lack of strength in the posterior chain are common deficiencies involved in squatting. Improving your clients' squat mechanics will enhance their ability to perform these activities and access their full functional capacity.

Pages 722 and 723 of the Exercise Professional's Guide to Personal Training shows appropriate progressions for improving squatting mechanics. Choosing these modifications depends on the current capability of your client.

- **Chair sit** great starting point for clients who struggle with stability, strength, and/or ROM.
- **Bodyweight squat**
- **Cable squat**
- **Barbell or weighted squat.**

Clients can exhibit *"lumbar dominance", "quad dominance",* or *"glute dominance"* during a squat. The glute-dominate squat pattern is preferred as it protects the lumbar spine and knees by reducing unnecessary stress on those areas. Ankle dorsiflexion is a major contributor to proper squat mechanics. The ability to properly *"hip hinge"* is also important. Encouraging clients to push their hips backwards *like they are sitting in a chair* before lowering into the squat will help reduce improper technique. Starting at the hips and allowing the knees to track with the ankle joint *typically aligned over the 2nd and 3rd toes* is a good cue. It's important to maintain a neutral spine during hinging and squatting and limit over flexion or extension of the lumbar area. Observe their squatting mechanics and correct any alignment issues. Look to see if they use their arms and upper body to compensate, and limit them from squatting deeper than their current ability.

Ankle and Lower Leg

Shin Splints is a general term used to describe exertional lower-leg pain. They most often occur due to an increased volume of activity that is unaccustomed *(running, dancing)* Shin splints are not the same as stress fractures, and oftentimes they do not require complete rest only modification of the exercise program *(lower impact, lower mileage).*

Stretching the calf muscles on the posterior chain can also be beneficial. ***Figure 15-37 on page 725 of the Exercise Professional's Guide*** shows the variation of standing calf stretches. A straight-leg calf stretch targets the gastrocnemius, a bent-leg calf stretch targets the soleus.

Ankle Sprains are common injuries that affect about 2 million people in the US each year. Most ankle sprains occur from inversion of the ankle *"rolling the ankle."* They are treated like any other sprain to allow the healing process to take place. A gradual return to activity as tolerated aiming to restore proprioception, flexibility, and strength once the injured area is ready.

Achilles Tendinitis is inflammation of the Achilles tendon connection at the heel of the foot. This often occurs from a quick take off from a static position. Like running from first to second base in a baseball game. The ability to dorsiflex the ankle is helpful to prevent and mitigate the potential for this condition. Although overstretching can flare up tendinitis. Gradual dynamic stretching of the calf muscles can help improve the elasticity of the posterior muscles and ROM of the ankle joint.

Plantar Fasciitis is an inflammation of the connective tissue on the bottom of the foot that runs from our heel bone to the toes. Stretching of the calf muscles and plantar fascia are helpful to relieve symptoms along with self-myofascial release with a tennis ball, lacrosse ball, or golf ball. I periodically use a standing desk with an ergonomic mat and keep a lacrosse ball close by to roll the bottom of my feet and also use the higher back portion of the mat to stretch my calves. This is a good option to keep the feet active and flexible if a standing desk is an option for a client's work environment.

The following steps can be followed to address and improve foot, ankle function.

- *First,* address mobility and stability in the foot and ankle
- *Next,* improve strength in the muscles that control movement in the sagittal plane.
- *Then,* improve strength in the muscles that control movement in the transverse and frontal planes.
- *Lastly,* improve strength in the muscles of the posterior chain.

The Healing Process

The body goes through three stages of healing when a soft-tissue injury occurs. Acute injuries can turn into chronic injuries if they are not cared for properly. The body needs time to cycle through the entire healing process. Repeated microtrauma to the area can cause a reoccurring chronic injury cycle. Rest and restricted activity is advised in the early stages, with movement as tolerated in the later phases. The goal is to maintain range of motion, and strength while decreasing scar tissue.

- ➤ **Phase I** *(Inflammation)*
  - ○ **Time**: First 3 – 4 days
  - ○ **Characteristics**: Redness, swelling, pain, and local heat.
  - ○ **Movement**: Non-weight bearing, active range of motion.

- ➤ **Phase II** *(Repair)*
  - ○ **Time**: Lasting 3 days – 6 weeks
  - ○ **Characteristics**: The injured area fills with collagen and other cells which will eventually form a scar.
  - ○ **Movement**: Weight-bearing as tolerated.

- ➤ **Phase III** *(Remodeling)*
  - ○ **Time**: Beginning 4 weeks – 2 years
  - ○ **Characteristics**: Increased strength of scar tissue by remodeling into a more organized structure.
  - ○ **Movement**: Progressive, pain-free exercise.

The following treatment should be used immediately after musculoskeletal injuries such as sprains, strains, bruises, and other soft-tissue injuries:

RICE: *Rest, Ice, Compression, and Elevation*

Table 15-3 on page 694 of the Exercise Professional's Guide to Personal Training shows Muscular and Cardiorespiratory Training Considerations for Post-rehabilitation. Modified exercise programs are appropriate for those with localized injuries. *For example, a client with an ankle sprain can still exercise the upper body and perform seated exercises that do not load the injured ankle.*

Acronym and Abbreviation Meanings

ABC's: *Airway, Breathing, Circulation, Severe bleeding (vital indicators in unresponsive person)*

ACE IFT: *ACE Integrated Fitness Training Model*

ACL: *Anterior Cruciate Ligament*

ADL: *Activities of Daily Living*

AED: *Automated External Defibrillator*

ANS: *Autonomic Nervous System*

ASIS: *Anterior Superior Iliac Spine*

ATP: *Adenosine Triphosphate (High energy compound required to do mechanical work)*

BMD: *Bone Mineral Density*

BMI: *Body Mass Index*

BMR: *Basal Metabolic Rate*

BOS: *Base of Support*

CAD: *Coronary Artery Disease*

CFS: *Chronic Fatigue Syndrome*

CNS: *Central Nervous System*

COG: *Center of Gravity*

COM: *Center of Mass*

CPR: *Cardiopulmonary Resuscitation*

CRF: *Cardiorespiratory Fitness*

CVD: *Cardiovascular Disease*

DBP: *Diastolic Blood Pressure*

DDD: *Degenerative Disc Disease*

DOMS: *Delayed Onset Muscle Soreness*

Acronym and Abbreviation Meanings

DUP: *Daily Undulating Periodization*

EFI: *Exercise-induced Feeling Inventory*

EPOC: *Excess Post Oxygen Consumption*

FIRST: *Frequency, Intensity, Repetitions, Sets, and Type*

FITT-VP: *Frequency, Intensity, Time, Type, Volume, and Progression*

GTO: *Golgi Tendon Organ*

GXT: *Graded Exercise Test*

HIIT: *High-Intensity Interval Training*

HRR: *Heart Rate Reserve* (Max HR - Resting HR)

IBW: *Ideal Body Weight*

LOG: *Line of Gravity*

LOS: *Limits of Stability*

MET: *Metabolic Energy Equivalent (3.5 ml) an index of energy expenditure*

MVC: *Maximal Voluntary Contraction*

OARS: *Open-ended questions, Affirmations, Reflective listening, and Summarizing.*

OBLA: *Onset of Blood Lactate Accumulation*

PAD: *Peripheral Arterial Disease*

PAR-Q: *Physical Activity Readiness Questionnaire*

PCr: *Creatine Phosphate*

PNF: *Proprioceptive Neuromuscular Facilitation*

PNS: *Peripheral Nervous System*

RCT: *Respiratory Compensation Threshold*

RDA: *Recommended Daily Amount*

Acronym and Abbreviation Meanings

RE-AIM: *Reach, Efficacy, Adoption, Implementation,* and *Maintenance*

RER: *Respiratory Exchange Ratio*

RHR: *Resting Heart Rate*

RICE: *Rest, Ice, Compression,* and *Elevation*

ROI: *Return on Investment*

ROM: *Range of Motion*

RMR: *Resting Metabolic Rate*

RPE: *Ratings of Perceived Exertion*

SAID: *Specific Adaptations to Imposed Demands*

SBP: *Systolic Blood Pressure*

SITS: *Supraspinatus, Infraspinatus, Teres minor, Subscapularis (Rotator Cuff Muscles)*

SMALL Goals: *Self-selected, Measurable, Action-oriented, Linked to your life* and *Long-term*

SMART Goals: *Specific, Measurable, Attainable, Relevant, Time-Bound*

SMR: *Self-Myofascial Release*

SOAP note: *Subjective, Objective, Assessment, Plan*

SSC: *Stretch Shortening Cycle*

SSRI: *Selective Serotonin Reuptake Inhibitors*

SWOT analysis: *Strengths, Weaknesses, Opportunities, Threats (Used for risk assessment)*

TIA: *Transient Ischemic Attack*

THR: *Target Heart Rate*

TTM: *The Transtheoretical Model*

TVA: *Transverse Abdominis*

WHR: *Waist to Hip Ratio*

Conversions

Fat = 9 calories per gram

Protein = 4 calories per gram

Carbohydrates = 4 calories per gram

Alcohol = 7 calories per gram

3500 kcal *(calories)* = 1 pound of fat

1 Kg = 2.2 pounds (pounds ÷ 2.2 = Kg)

1 Inch = 2.54 cm (inches x 2.54 = cm)

1 Meter = 100 cm (cm ÷ 100 = Meters)

1 MET = 3.5 ml (VO$_2$ ÷ 3.5 = MET)

Formulas

Max Heart Rate (MHR): 220 – Age = MHR or 208 – (0.7 x Age) = MHR
* *30-year-old would have Max HR of 190 BPM | 220 – 30 = 190 BPM*

Heart Rate Reserve (HRR): Max HR – Resting HR = HRR
* *30-year-old with resting HR of 60 BPM | 190 - 60 = 130 BPM*

Target Heart Rate (THR) = HRR x % Intensity + Resting HR *(Karvonen Formula)*
* *30-year-old mentioned above to train at 80% intensity | 130 x 0.80 + 60 = 164 BPM (THR)*

Body Mass Index (BMI) = Weight (Kg) ÷ Height (m^2)
* *Calculate the BMI of a man who is 6ft tall and weighs 180 pounds*
180 ÷ 2.2 = 81.81 Kg | 6ft x 12 = 72 inches |72 x 2.54 = 182.88 cm | 182.88 ÷ 100 = 1.83 m
|1.83m^2 = 3.35 | 81.81 ÷ 3.35 = 24.42 BMI

Fat weight (FW) = Body weight (BW) x Body fat (BF) %
* *Calculate based on 180-pound body weight and 20% body fat | 180 x 0.20 = 36 lbs of fat*

Lean body weight (LBW) = Body weight (BW) – Fat weight (FW)
* *Calculate based on information above | 180 – 36 = 144 lbs LBW*

Desired Body Weight (DBW) = Lean body weight ÷ (100% - Desired body fat %)
* *Calculate DBW if the person above wanted to be at 10% body fat | 144 ÷ 0.90 = 160 lbs*

Waist to Hip Ratio (WHR) = Waist circumference ÷ Hip circumference
* *Calculate based on an individual with a 32-inch waist and 36-inch hip | 32 ÷ 36 = 0.89*

1 Repetition Max (1RM) = Pounds lifted ÷ % of 1RM (See <u>1RM Table</u> for % 1RM based on reps)
* *Calculate based on 180 pounds lifted for 10 repetitions | 180 ÷ 0.75 = 240 pounds 1RM*

Total calories from fat (FAT CAL) = Fat grams per serving x 9 kcal x # of servings per container

Percent of calories from fat (%FAT) = (Fat grams per serving x 9 kcal) ÷ Calories per serving

Calculation for daily caloric deficit to achieve desired weight loss in a set timeframe

   ➤ **Weekly caloric deficit** = (Desired weight loss in pounds x 3500) ÷ # of weeks

   ➤ **Daily caloric deficit** = Weekly caloric deficit ÷ 7

Practice Questions

1) The *"Talk Test"* describes when a person can talk comfortably in sentences while performing an exercise. This is a good indicator that someone is training in _____ for Cardiorespiratory Training?

    A. Zone 1 *(Base Training)*
    B. Zone 2 *(Fitness Training)*
    C. Zone 3 *(Performance Training)*
    D. None of the Above

2) Movement training is the second phase of muscular training for the ACE IFT Model. What are the *Five Primary Movement Patterns* that are incorporated in this phase of training?

    A. Bench Press, Single-leg, Pushing, Pulling, and Retraction
    B. Bend-and-lift, Single-leg, Pushing, Planking, and Rotational
    C. Deadlift, Squatting, Pushing, Pulling, and Rotational
    D. Bend-and-lift, Single-leg, Pushing, Pulling, and Rotational

3) Which of the following movements does an overhead press exercise BEST mimic?

    A. Picking up a child
    B. Opening a door
    C. Picking an object up off the ground
    D. Putting a box on a high shelf

4) During load training, it is recommended to increase the resistance by _____ once the end range repetitions are achieved in order to provide progressive overload and facilitate further strength development.

    A. 3%
    B. 5%
    C. 7%
    D. 10%

5) Which of the following musculoskeletal injuries describes a sprain?

   A. A stretching or tearing of muscles or tendons.
   B. Pain in the front of the knee.
   C. A stretching or tearing of ligaments.
   D. Inflammation of a tendon and/or tendon-muscle attachment.

6) What is the recommended minimum weekly amount of exercise for the general population?

   A. 300 Minutes
   B. 200 Minutes
   C. 150 Minutes
   D. 250 Minutes

7) "Only the muscles that are trained will adapt and change in response." BEST describes which of the following training principles?

   A. Overload
   B. Specificity
   C. Reversibility
   D. Periodization

8) Daniel is 6ft tall and weighs 180 pounds, what is his BMI calculation?

   A. 23.45
   B. 22.42
   C. 25.45
   D. 24.42

9) BMI cannot determine actual body composition, which means it can unfairly categorize which of the following types of individuals?

   A. A person with a lot of body fat.
   B. An ectomorph with little muscle and body fat
   C. A person with a lot of muscle mass.
   D. None of the above.

10) Marie wants to lose 12 pounds by her wedding day which is 15 weeks away. Which of the following daily caloric deficits would be MOST effective to achieve her goal safely?

   A. 200 kcals caloric deficit combined with 200 kcals burned thru activity per day
   B. 500 kcals caloric deficit combined with 200 kcals burned thru activity per day
   C. 300 kcals caloric deficit combined with 300 kcals burned thru activity per day
   D. 200 kcals caloric deficit combined with 100 kcals burned thru activity per day

11) Joe is currently 200 pounds with a body fat percentage of 20%. He would like to reduce his body fat percentage to 14%. What would Joe's body weight be at the reduced body fat percentage?

   A. 181 pounds
   B. 176 pounds
   C. 190 pounds
   D. 186 pounds

12) There are 24 individual vertebrae in the spine. How many vertebrae make up the lumbar portion of the spine?

   A. 12
   B. 7
   C. 5
   D. 9

13) Mike recently had a physical check-up that was required by his employer. The physician recommended that Mike quit smoking and begin an exercise program to reduce his high cholesterol and high blood pressure. His employer paid for exercise sessions at the gym near their office. Mike expresses to the personal trainer that he is only there so he will not lose his job. Using the Transtheoretical Model what stage of change is Mike currently in?

   A. Contemplation
   B. Action
   C. Preparation
   D. Pre-contemplation

14) Which of the following describes proper positioning during the bend and lift screen?

    A. Tibia and torso are parallel to each other in the lowered position.

    B. Knees are lined up over the ankles in the lowered position.

    C. Quadriceps are parallel to the floor in the lowered position.

    D. None of the above

15) When a client is learning a new skill or exercise which stage of learning requires the MOST feedback from the personal trainer?

    A. Cognitive

    B. Associative

    C. Autonomous

    D. Assertive

16) A personal trainer demonstrates proper exercise technique for the deadlift to a client while verbally describing the necessary movement pattern. After the client performs the exercise they ask the personal trainer to explain it again. What type of learner BEST describes this client?

    A. Visual

    B. Kinesthetic

    C. Evaluative

    D. Auditory

17) A client has recently missed multiple workout sessions. They have just started a new job that is further away from the gym and finding time to exercise has been difficult. They express frustration to their trainer. What is the MOST appropriate response the personal trainer can give?

    A. "You should prioritize your life and make time for exercise without excuses."

    B. "I understand your frustration; lapses are a normal part of the process. Let's create an exercise plan that better fits your new schedule."

    C. "Consistency is key to achieving your goals; you must make time for exercise in order to achieve them."

    D. "It's OK, let's just try to exercise more during your free time."

18) When exercising in a hot outside environment a client shows the following symptoms: High body temperature, dry red skin, rapid strong pulse. Which of the following conditions are they MOST likely experiencing?

    A. Heat stroke
    B. Heat edema
    C. Heat exhaustion
    D. Heat cramps

19) What is the recommended fluid intake amount post-exercise?

    A. 17 – 20 ounces for every pound of weight lost
    B. 7 – 10 ounces for every pound of weight lost
    C. 16 – 24 ounces for every pound of weight lost
    D. 10 – 20 ounces for every pound of weight lost

20) A regular client has recently changed to a calorie-restricted diet that does not include consuming animal protein. Although they have reached their goal weight, they explain to their trainer that they feel weak and fatigued during workouts and ask them for advice. Which of the following responses should the personal trainer give?

    A. "You should supplement your diet with a complete protein such as whey protein powder to eliminate the fatigue you are feeling."
    B. "I know a great natural supplement company that has products to help increase energy. I will get you their information after our session."
    C. "You should take vitamin B12 to increase your energy levels."
    D. "I know a great dietician who can give you advice. I will get you their contact information after our session."

21) A client notes on a Health-history questionnaire that they are currently taking beta-blocker medication for hypertension *(high blood pressure)*. Which of the following methods of estimating exercise intensity should be used with this type of client?

    A. Target Heart Rate (THR) using the Karvonen Formula
    B. Metabolic Energy Equivalents (MET)
    C. Ratings of Perceived Exertion (RPE)
    D. Target VO_2 using a percentage of their VO_2 Max

22) The majority of people's communication is obtained by which of the following means?

    A. Verbal
    B. Nonverbal
    C. Listening
    D. Description

23) What is the recommended amount of time for the Warm-up period before exercise?

    A. At least 10 – 20 minutes
    B. At least 5 – 20 minutes
    C. At least 10 – 15 minutes
    D. At least 5 – 10 minutes

24) Tim is able to bench press 180 pounds for 10 repetitions. What is his predicted One Repetition Max (1RM) weight?

    A. 250 pounds
    B. 240 pounds
    C. 230 pounds
    D. 260 pounds

25) Which of the following exercise strategies is MOST effective for increasing power?

    A. Controlled slow repetitions with moderate resistance
    B. High-velocity low repetitions with moderate resistance
    C. Heavy resistance with slow repetitions
    D. Low-velocity high repetitions with light resistance

26) A personal trainer notices that one of the pedals on an elliptical machine has a screw missing and is unstable. What is the appropriate procedure to follow in this situation?

    A. Notify the facility's management and unplug the machine.
    B. Put a note on the machine to let people know it is defective.
    C. Notify the facility's management and block off that area until it has been addressed.
    D. Notify the other members in the gym so they don't use the machine.

27) Which of the following exercises would BEST target the pectoralis major muscles?

    A. Pull-ups

    B. Overhead press

    C. Bodyweight push-ups

    D. Bench dips

28) The movement of the overhead shoulder press takes place in which plane of motion?

    A. Frontal

    B. Sagittal

    C. Transverse

    D. Horizontal

29) What is the optimal spotting position for the personal trainer when their client is performing an overhead dumbbell press?

    A. Behind the client with hands placed on or near their elbows

    B. In front of the client with hands placed on the weight.

    C. Behind the client with hands placed on or near their wrist below the weight.

    D. Behind the client with hands placed on the weight.

30) Which of the following sources of information would have the MOST influence on a client's self-efficacy who has just started an exercise program to lose weight?

    A. Another client's success story of losing weight.

    B. Their own past performance experience with exercise.

    C. Encouragement from their trainer.

    D. Self-appraisal of current fitness level.

31) What joint actions occur during the concentric portion of a deadlift?

    A. Knee extension, Hip flexion

    B. Knee flexion, Hip flexion

    C. Knee extension, Hip extension

    D. Knee flexion, Hip extension

32) Which of the following make up the hamstring muscle complex?

    A. Rectus femoris, Vastus lateralis, Vastus intermedius, Vastus medialis
    B. Biceps femoris (long and short heads), Semitendinosus, Semimembranosus
    C. Supraspinatus, Infraspinatus, Teres minor, Subscapularis
    D. Rectus abdominis, Gastrocnemius, Soleus, Calcaneus

33) If a person stands with ankle pronation, their knees will be _____?

    A. Internally rotated
    B. Neutral to the line of gravity
    C. Externally rotated
    D. Supinated

34) A client states that they have been experiencing neck and jaw pain that radiates to their left arm. What should the personal trainer do in this situation?

    A. Do some neck stretches at the end of their session to relieve tension in that area.
    B. Refer them to a physical therapist that can help alleviate the pain.
    C. Explain to them the implications of a possible heart attack and refer them to their physician for treatment and clearance to resume exercise.
    D. Recommend they take a few days off from exercising and take Advil for the pain.

35) During a static posture assessment, a trainer notices the client stands with internally rotated shoulders and a rounded *(slouched)* back. What BEST describes this postural deviation?

    A. Lordosis
    B. Scoliosis
    C. Kyphosis
    D. Flat Back

36) A person with Lordosis would likely have which of the following muscle imbalances?

    A. Tight hip flexors and erector spinae, Weak abdominals, and hip extensors
    B. Weak hip flexors and erector spinae, Tight abdominals, and hip extensors
    C. Tight hip flexors and abdominals, Weak erector spinae, and hip extensors
    D. Weak hip flexors and abdominals, Tight erector spinae, and hip extensors

37) What form must be obtained from a client prior to performing assessments?

    A. Waiver

    B. Informed consent

    C. Client-trainer agreement

    D. Contract

38) Which of the following would be a contraindicated exercise for a client who has osteoporosis?

    A. Leg press at high-intensity (8-RM)

    B. Using an elliptical at moderate intensity

    C. Double leg V-ups

    D. Planks

39) Exercising for the enjoyment and long-term health benefits describes which type of motivation?

    A. Social

    B. Extrinsic

    C. Environmental

    D. Intrinsic

40) Muscles that act primarily as stabilizers generally contain greater concentrations of which type of muscle fibers?

    A. Type I *(slow-twitch)*

    B. Type II *(fast-twitch)*

    C. Type IIx *(intermediate)*

    D. Sarcomeres

41) What muscle acts as a stabilizer during the push-up?

    A. Latissimus dorsi

    B. Triceps

    C. Rectus abdominis

    D. Pectoralis major

42) When should a client's heart rate be checked during a cycle ergometer test?

    A. One minute after the test has been completed.
    B. One minute before and one minute after the test has been completed.
    C. Continually minute by minute during the test.
    D. Immediately after the test has been completed.

43) Which of the following should a personal trainer be aware of when working with a client who is on diuretics to maintain their high blood pressure?

    A. Dehydration
    B. Dyslipidemia
    C. Sinus bradycardia
    D. Claudication

44) Which blood pressure measurement is likely to decrease slightly or remain unchanged during exercise?

    A. Systolic blood pressure
    B. Diastolic blood pressure
    C. Resting blood pressure
    D. None of the above

45) Which muscle fiber type is best suited for Olympic style lifters?

    A. Type IIx *(intermediate)*
    B. Type I *(slow-twitch)*
    C. Type II *(fast-twitch)*
    D. None of the above

46) Jane is a 35-year-old with a resting heart rate of 50 BPM. What would her target heart rate be if she is looking to train at 80% intensity of her heart rate reserve (HRR)?

    A. 148 BPM
    B. 153 BPM
    C. 158 BPM
    D. 151 BPM

47) What is the smallest contractile unit of a muscle fiber that is responsible for the striated appearance of muscle tissue?

  A. Muscle spindle
  B. Sarcomere
  C. Myosin *(thick filament)*
  D. Actin *(thin filament)*

48) Restoring proper muscle length-tension relationships are essential to good posture and functional movement patterns. What would be the appropriate action to correct postural kyphosis in a client?

  A. Stretch the upper back *(trapezius)* and strengthen the chest *(pectoralis muscles)*
  B. Strengthen the hip flexors and stretch the hip extensors
  C. Strengthen the upper back *(trapezius)* and stretch the chest *(pectoralis muscles)*
  D. Stretch the hip flexors and strengthen the hip extensors

49) Which of the following describes Absolute Contraindication?

  A. The benefits of exercise outweigh the risk. Exercise testing can be done only after careful evaluation of the risk/benefit ratio.
  B. The risks of exercise testing outweigh the potential benefit. The client should not participate in exercise testing until conditions are stabilized or treated.
  C. The risk/benefit of exercise testing is even. Exercise testing can be done only after careful evaluation of the risk/benefit ratio.
  D. None of the above

50) A personal trainer notices a person lying motionless on the floor in the locker room of their fitness facility. What is the FIRST thing the personal trainer should do in this situation?

  A. Call or tell someone to call for help.
  B. Immediately begin CPR and have someone prep the AED.
  C. Check their vital indicators ABC: *Airway, Breathing, Circulation*
  D. None of the above.

Practice Question Answers

1) **A** / Zone 1 *(Base Training)* Involves low to moderate exercise that reflects heart rates below the ***talk test*** ventilatory threshold 1.

2) **D** / Bend-and-lift, Single-leg, Pushing, Pulling, and Rotational.

3) **D** / Putting a box on a high shelf.

4) **B** / 5% is the recommended increase when adding resistance.

5) **C** / A stretching or tearing of ligaments.

6) **C** / 150 minutes is the minimum weekly amount of exercise recommended.

7) **B** / Specificity

8) **D** / 24.42 | Body Mass Index (BMI) = Weight in Kg ÷ Height in m^2 (meters squared) | 180 ÷ 2.2 = 81.81 Kg | 6ft x 12 = 72 inches |72 x 2.54 = 182.88 (1 inch = 2.54 cm) | 182.88 ÷ 100 = 1.83 (1 Meter = 100 cm) |1.83^2 = 3.35 | 81.81 ÷ 3.35 = 24.42 BMI

9) **C** / A person with a lot of muscle mass.

10) **A** / 200 kcals caloric deficit combined with 200 kcals burned thru activity per day 15 weeks x 7 days a week = 105 days total | 12 pounds x 3500 *(calories per pound of fat)* = 42,000 calories to burn | 42,000 ÷ 105 = 400 calories per day deficit is required to lose 12 pounds in 15 weeks.

11) **D** / 186 pounds | Desired Body Weight = Lean body weight ÷ (100% - Desired body fat %)| 200 x 0.20 = 40 pounds of fat | 200 − 40 = 160 pounds of LBW | 160 ÷ (1.00 − 0.14) | 160 ÷ 0.86 = 186 pounds

12) **C** / 5 vertebrae make up the lumbar portion of the spine.

13) **D** / Pre-contemplation

14) **A** / Tibia and torso are parallel to each other in the lowered position.

15) **B** / Associative

16) **D** / Auditory

17) **B** / "I understand your frustration; lapses are a normal part of the process. Let's create an exercise plan that better fits your new schedule."

18) **A** / Heat stroke

19) **C** / 16 – 24 ounces for every pound of weight lost.

20) **D** / "I know a great dietician who can give you advice. I will get you their contact information after our session."

21) **C** / Ratings of Perceived Exertion (RPE)

22) **B** / Nonverbal

23) **D** / At least 5 – 10 minutes

24) **B** / 240 pounds | 180 ÷ 0.75 = 240lbs 1RM | See <u>1RM Table</u> for % 1RM based on reps

25) **B** / High-velocity low repetitions with moderate resistance.

26) **C** / Notify the facility's management and block off that area until it has been addressed.

27) **C** / Bodyweight push-ups

28) **A** / Frontal

29) **C** / Behind the client with hands placed on or near their wrist below the weight.

30) **B** / Their own past performance experience with exercise.

31) **C** / Knee extension, Hip extension

32) **B** / Biceps femoris *(long and short heads),* Semitendinosus, Semimembranosus

33) **A** / Internally rotated

34) **C** / Explain to them the implications of a possible heart attack and refer them to their physician for treatment and clearance to resume exercise.

35) **C** / Kyphosis

36) **A** / Tight hip flexors and erector spinae, Weak abdominals, and hip extensors

37) **B** / Informed consent

38) **C** / Double leg V-ups

39) **D** / Intrinsic motivation comes from within *(internal)* not external sources.

40) **A** / Type I *(slow-twitch/endurance)* muscle fibers are better suited for stabilizer muscles

41) **C** / Rectus abdominis

42) **C** / Continually minute by minute during the test.

43) **A** / Dehydration

44) **B** / Diastolic blood pressure

45) **C** / Type II *(fast-twitch)* muscles fibers are better suited for explosive Olympic style lifts

46) **C** / 158 BPM | Target Heart Rate = Max HR - Resting HR x % of Intensity + Resting HR
220-35 = 185 Max Heart Rate | 185-50 x 0.80 + 50 = 158 BPM

47) **B** / Sarcomere

48) **C** / Strengthen the upper back *(trapezius)* and stretch the chest *(pectoralis muscles)*

49) **B** / The risks of exercise testing outweigh the potential benefit. The client should not participate in exercise testing until conditions are stabilized or treated.

50) **C** / Check their vital indicators ABC: *Airway, Breathing, Circulation.*

Resources and Helpful Links

ACE Exam Content Outline

www.acefitness.org/fitness-certifications/pdfs/CPT-Exam-Content-Outline.pdf

ACE Certification Handbook

www.acefitness.org/fitness-certifications/pdfs/Certification-Exam-Candidate-Handbook.pdf

ACE Code of Ethics

www.acefitness.org/fitness-certifications/certified-code.aspx

ACE Study Center (Facebook)

www.facebook.com/ACEFitnessAnswers

Personal Trainer Resources / Anatomy / Assessments / Training Principles / Blog

www.cptprep.com/single-post/resources

ACE CPT Prep / Functional Assessments / Blog

www.cptprep.com/blog/1-14-18

Overactive / Underactive Muscles / Everything you need to know / Blog

www.cptprep.com/blog/9-21-18

New Preparticipation Guidelines

www.acefitness.org/education-and-resources/professional/certified/february-2018/6898/new-preparticipation-guidelines-remove-barriers-to-exercise

New Blood Pressure Guidelines

www.acefitness.org/education-and-resources/professional/certified/july-2018/7042/what-the-new-blood-pressure-guidelines-mean-to-you?

ACE Exam Prep Blog

www.acefitness.org/blogs/2/exam-preparation-blog

ACE Tools and Calculators

www.acefitness.org/acefit/tools-and-calculators

Test Taking Strategies

www.acefitness.org/blog/5305/set-yourself-up-for-success-with-these-test-taking

Nutrition Scope of Practice for ACE Fitness Professionals

www.acefitness.org/certifiednews/images/article/pdfs/NutritionScopeOfPractice.pdf

Thank You!

I want to personally thank you for choosing this study guide to prepare for the ACE CPT Exam. I enjoy gathering and sharing information that I have found useful and getting feedback from those who have used our products. If you found this helpful, I would greatly appreciate you taking a quick minute to leave a review by scanning the QR code below with a smartphone camera. It helps us continue to make the best products possible and pays it forward to others letting them know what to expect.

Becoming a certified personal trainer is a journey just like any other endeavor in life. You will learn and adapt along the way. CPT Prep's company logo is a chevron symbol that means to **"Create your own Path"** which if you are reading this you have already started.

I wish you all the best with your future endeavors as a fitness professional!

Daniel Hile

~ CPT Exam Prep Team

Study while on the go with ACE Audio Prep! It's a great supplement to this study guide that goes chapter-by-chapter pointing out all of the key information. Available on Amazon, Audible, and iTunes. Scan the QR code below with a smartphone camera to begin listening ↓

Follow us @CPTPrep
Contact info@cptprep.com

Access additional tips and resources at www.cptprep.com

<u>References</u>

1) *The Exercise Professional's Guide to Personal Training.*